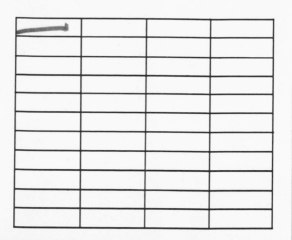

HT
391
.R383
1980

R   crisis

D1067471

REGIONS IN CRISIS

Regions in Crisis

New Perspectives in European Regional Theory

Edited by
John Carney, Ray Hudson and Jim Lewis

ST. MARTIN'S PRESS NEW YORK

Printed in Great Britain
First published in the United States in 1980

Library of Congress Cataloging in Publication Data
Main entry under title:

Regions in crisis.

   Bibliography: p. 167.
   Includes index.
   1. Regional economics—Addresses, essays, lectures.
2. Regional planning—European Economic Community
countries—Addresses, essays, lectures. I. Carney, John,
1948-   II. Hudson, Raymond.   III. Lewis, Jim.
HT391.R383   1980   330.9   79-3836

ISBN 0-312-66944-5

CONTENTS

FIGURES

TABLES

PREFACE

It is our contention that, since the onset of the international recession in 1973, regional problems and regional crises have become the major underlying disintegrative tendency in the EEC. Partly in response to this surprising turn of events, new perspectives in regional theory have begun to be firmly established in most European countries. The main aims of our book are to introduce these new perspectives and to make important contributions accessible to an English-speaking audience. The papers in the book have, however, also been selected so as to deal with some of the most crucial contemporary regional problems and regional crisis tendencies in Europe.

Four of the papers were specially translated for the book, three from French and one from Dutch. In preparing the translations from French we had invaluable help from Mr R. Firth of Newcastle University Library. The translation from Dutch was completed with the assistance of Ben Janssen and Sef Slootweg of Nijmegen University. Mrs D.M. Carney translated Italian material and commented on the other translations. Alain Lipietz also kindly made comments on our draft translation of his paper.

For permission to publish our translations we are grateful to the authors concerned and to the editors and publishers of: *Environment and Planning, Economie et Politique* and *Zone*. Chapter 3 was first published in French in *Environment and Planning*, A, vol. 7 (1975) and Chapter 4 was originally published in *Economie et Politique*, nos. 237-8 (1974). Chapter 5 is a modified version of a paper first published in *Economie et Politique*, nos. 264-5 (1976). Chapter 6, which was revised for this collection, was originally published in *Zone*, no. 5 (1977). An earlier version of Chapter 2 was published in P.W.J. Batey (ed.), *Theory and Method in Urban and Regional Analysis* (Pion, London, 1978). The views expressed in these chapters are those of the authors and are not necessarily those of the editors.

We are grateful to those members of the Regional Science Association (British Section), Regional Social Theory Workshop who made critical comments on the manuscript. We would like to thank Pieter van Hoogstraten and Dave Etherington for their help in choosing references for inclusion in Chapter 7 and secretarial and cartographic staff in Durham for their assistance with the manuscript. Ray Hudson would also like to acknowledge financial assistance from the University of Durham which enabled him to travel to Italy in 1978.

Since the start of 1979, the political importance of regional problems has been dramatically underlined by events in France, where the State has been severely shaken by a major upsurge of popular protest in Lorraine and the Nord. These events have been the clearest expression yet of the possible social and political consequences of regional crises which are maturing in many more parts of Europe and which could erupt with great force and suddenness at any time.

John Carney
Ray Hudson
Jim Lewis
Durham

1 NEW PERSPECTIVES IN EUROPEAN REGIONAL THEORY: SOME INTRODUCTORY REMARKS

John Carney, Ray Hudson and Jim Lewis

Background

New departures in European regional theory began to be established in the early 1960s in the wake of Myrdal's critique of neo-classical growth theories.[1] However, it was not until the end of the sixties that thoroughly distinctive new perspectives were established.[2] Regional problems, as conventionally defined, started to be re-interpreted using theories of capital accumulation as a reference point. Regional problems, investment location processes and uneven regional development came to be regarded as necessary pre-conditions for or inescapable consequences of accumulation imperatives operating on a world scale.

This book includes chapters which illustrate the issues addressed as the new perspectives in European regional theory evolved in the seventies, a period when regional problems and regional crisis tendencies in Europe grew considerably in scale and intensity. Each chapter is in some way concerned with the analysis of the regional and locational consequences of accumulation imperatives. There are, however, several differences between the papers in the specific concepts and interpretations put forward. For this reason, this chapter aims to elucidate some of the most distinctive contributions or points made in each chapter and to examine three issues of considerable importance to the further evolution of European regional theory. The chapter concludes by referring to possible contexts within which regional theory will be further elaborated in the 1980s.

The New Perspectives

Regional Problems and the Spatial Division of Labour

Alain Lipietz (in Chapter 3) argues that it is necessary to consider the articulation of modes of production as a starting-point for analysing contemporary regional problems.[3] Using the example of the historical articulation of petty commodity production and capitalism, Lipietz suggests that regions specialised in petty commodity production have experienced two successive phases of domination. The first is called '*external domination*', in which 'small, independent producers or small and medium-sized local capitalists carry on an unequal exchange with the dominant region by means of the price of commodities.' This unequal exchange is a block on autonomous capitalist development in the region affected and prepares the way for a second phase, '*integration-domination*', where external capital takes direct control of local production.

Once established, the articulation of petty commodity production and capitalism tends to open up an increasing gap between dominant and dominated regions. The result is the establishment and enlarged reproduction of a centre-periphery spatial structure in which two forms of accumulation occur. 'Self-centred' accumulation operates in central regions and 'extraverted accumulation' in peripheral regions.

The growth of multinational companies has been indispensable to the growth of late capitalism as a whole.[4] Lipietz is arguing that this growth could not have been achieved and, by implication, could not be maintained in future, without the existence of this fundamental polaris-ation of spatial structure, the development of which has been accelera-ted by multinationals but which is also dependent on State intervention.

Lipietz contends that the establishment of the *branch circuit* as a form of economic organisation is vital to the expansion of multi-national capital and that, in turn, branch circuits are founded upon international and inter-regional divisions of labour based upon the fundamental centre-periphery polarisation of international economic space into regions of self-centred accumulation and extraverted accumulation.

Branch circuits depend upon the existence and reproduction of three types of economic region: (1) those with 'a highly technological environment' where a skilled labour supply is crucial; (2) regions with a high proportion of skilled personnel but lacking a diverse, modern industrial structure; and (3) regions which contain unskilled labour reserves 'produced by the dissolution of other modes or by the decline of obsolete industries corresponding to an earlier stage in the division of labour'.

Regions of type 3 generally have a history of extraverted accumula-tion. Branch circuit industrialisation does nothing to alter this situation. In fact it may actually reinforce the process and hence the centre-periphery polarisation of economic space.[5]

Lipietz argues that only concerted action or public initiative can ensure the continual restructuring of space required by monopoly capital. State action is also necessary to remove barriers to capitalist development arising from the legal ownership of space and earlier or

non-capitalist uses. Under competitive conditions capitalists are forced
to pay owners 'tribute' for the right to use land. Monopoly capital uses
State intervention to destroy this system.

On these grounds, Lipietz distinguished two important forms of
State intervention. The first acts so as to 'make up for the lack of a
law of value in space' through spatial planning and infrastructure
provision.[6] The second takes place in order to 'impose capitalist logic
on the inadequate framework of legal space'. Lipietz contends that
private capital alone 'cannot assure the regulation of its own extended
spatial development', hence State involvement in spatial planning. By
implication, Lipietz also suggests that the coexistence of the most
advanced forms of capitalist development with the remnants of other
earlier periods of capitalist development and of other modes of production depends on the capacity of the State to promote advanced
capitalism at the expense of all other interests.

As soon as 'internal and international evolution make it necessary',
the State is assigned the role of controlling and encouraging the establishment of a new inter-regional division of labour. The requirements of
monopoly capital for locational rearrangements then come into 'more
or less violent conflict with inherited space'. The State, therefore, seeks
to organise political and social interventions, especially in peripheral
regions, so as to win the support of local bourgeoisies for modernisation
programmes and to control social unrest occasioned by their implementation. The State also engages in modifications of space through zoning
provisions and seeks to establish the infrastructural capacity required
by monopoly capital. Territorial space is, therefore, in Lipietz's view, a
product of the complex relationships between monopoly capital,
State interventions and the spatial inheritances left over from earlier
periods of capitalist production or even from pre-capitalist modes of
production.

Regional Uneven Development

Dieter Läpple and Pieter van Hoogstraten (in Chapter 6) address some
of the issues considered by Lipietz. However, they approach the
analysis of regional uneven development from a rather different theoretical starting-point. They do not adhere to an Althusserian vocabulary
and reject the use of analogies drawn from international underdevelopment theory as a means of analysing regional problems in the advanced
capitalist countries. Nevertheless, like Lipietz, Läpple and Hoogstraten
aim to analyse uneven spatial development as a 'constituent moment in
the social process of development'. They also stress, like Lipietz, that

'the spatial structure of the process of reproduction' must be analysed as a result of capitalist relations of production. Uneven spatial development is reproduced due to 'the immanent tendencies of capitalist accumulation'.

Läpple and Hoogstraten define capitalist accumulation as 'a process of continuous expansion of surplus-value production and as a process of incorporation of the surplus value appropriated by the capitalist into the continuously increasing amount of capital'. To continue to exist, the capitalist mode of production must produce pre-conditions for its own continuity and expansion. This necessitates a perpetual increase in the productivity of social labour which, in turn, is only possible through an increase in the scale of social production, itself dependent on the expansion of individual capitals, an inherently uneven process, involving the centralisation and concentration of capital in value terms.

The existence of semi- or pre-capitalist relations of production within an advanced capitalist economy can reinforce uneven development but cannot be the prime motive for it. This must be immanent in the accumulation process itself. For this reason, they emphasise the importance of centralisation and concentration processes which lead to the systematic differentiation of capital and capitalist growth.

They argue that increases in labour productivity are only possible on the basis of the spatial concentration of labour power and of the means of production. Since increased productivity is essential to continued accumulation, spatial centralisation tendencies are usually predominant in the capitalist mode of production. Decentralisation tendencies are regarded as being comparatively weaker processes and Läpple and Hoogstraten contend that spatial concentration has actually increased as a response to the international recession.

The importance of spatial concentration tendencies is certainly evident in the case of the Netherlands where the 'historically determined spatial structure' has been reproduced with 'astonishing continuity'. However, it is by no means correct to suppose that decentralisation processes have been negligible in production restructuring, even in the Netherlands. On the contrary, it is clear that these processes have been important in most advanced European economies and were crucial in shaping uneven national and regional development in Italy.[7]

Nevertheless, it is also true that accounts of decentralisation and the consequent industrialisation of regional labour reserves often neglect to point out that gains in competitiveness resulting from these strategies are not chiefly due to enhanced productivity. They arise primarily from direct reductions in wage bills made possible because of the social conditions found in labour reserve regions. The possibility of perpetual gains in productivity is sacrificed in order temporarily to control wage costs and labour flexibility. Although units of capital in some sectors are able to take advantage of this option, in many sectors decentralisation is not a viable strategy. In these sectors locational concentration on an ever-increasing scale is essential for continued survival and for this reason huge *territorial production complexes* have begun to be established to organise 'chains of production' essential to general accumulation. These complexes have involved the concentration of unprecedented volumes of fixed capital which have grown at much faster rates than the volume of employment generated in the complexes.

Läpple and Hoogstraten argue that such a high degree of socialisation is necessary to produce these complexes that they cannot be created by way of the 'spontaneously and anarchistically functioning mechanism of price and profit'. However, the output of the complexes is vital to accumulation. In consequence, direct intervention by the State to provide land-use planning, infrastructure and co-ordinating services becomes unavoidable, a conclusion also put forward by Lipietz in Chapter 3 and by Damette in Chapter 4.

Regional Problems, Monopoly Exploitation and Investment Location Processes

Damette argues that the new trends in industrial location that have become established, since the mid-sixties, in all the advanced European economies are the consequence of general accumulation imperatives operating in the international economy: 'The dominant feature of the capitalist economies at the crisis stage of State Monopoly Capitalism is their increasing integration, in various forms, in world competition which is constantly becoming more severe.'

Due to these circumstances, individual units of capital are forced to seek out opportunities for obtaining 'surplus profits' and one way to do this is to discover ways of raising the rate of exploitation. Hence the search for reserves of labour 'which provide big capital with conditions for the super-exploitation of workers'. Geographical conditions which have the potential to allow super-exploitation to be achieved represent untapped sources of surplus profits.

However, in Damette's account, the search for reserves of labour and possibilities of raising the rate of exploitation constitutes an unstable system. Capital constantly seeks out new areas with the potential for super-exploitation and is always ready to abandon areas and sectors which no longer have this potential. Regional crises arise as a direct result.

Basic labour reserves are not necessarily automatically produced or reproduced by the workings of the market. State involvement is required to create conditions that permit super-exploitation on the scale dictated by the pressures of international competition. Damette's interpretation of this involvement is very precise: 'The central problem in spatial planning is to offer monopolies the optimal spatial conditions for maximising profits.' The State is seen as an instrument for regulating economic and social conditions in the interests of monopoly capital. State intervention is seen as being essential to the establishment and reproduction of basic labour reserves with characteristics suited to the requirements of the monopolies. These reserves must be *specialised* so that monopolies can plan their labour recruitment but also subject to control so that inter-firm competition does not arise leading to wage-cost inflation. The reserves must also be *diffused* so as to avoid the 'dangers' to profits of spatial concentration. Through urban policy and housing policy State intervention can reproduce labour reserves with these characteristics and in France regional planning focused on medium-sized towns has achieved considerable success in establishing basic reserves.

However, State intervention cannot eliminate the inherent instability of location tendencies in advanced capitalist economies. Capital has now become *hypermobile*; there has been an acceleration in the rate of obsolescence of industrial locations. State intervention either creates conditions which further accentuate hypermobility or is designed to alleviate its social costs in abandoned locations. In Damette's view chaos is, therefore, an *integral* and *permanent* feature of State Monopoly Capitalism. Moreover, the hypermobility of capital is a consequence of general accumulation imperatives operating at an international level.

Regional Crisis and Crisis Formation

As the international recession has deepened, hypermobility has accelerated as individual units of capital seek ways of adjusting to increasingly fierce international competition. For this reason, Damette and Poncet (in Chapter 5) argue that while regional crises ultimately reflect general crisis tendencies, there is also a distinct, specifically regional aspect to crisis formation.

They show that even in periods of rapid economic growth, regional crises may continue to exist. Regional crisis tendencies are, however, more easily contained and managed when there is an 'undertone of expansion' in national and international economies. Since the mid-sixties, international competition has become much stronger as an 'undertone of contraction' has gathered force. Damette and Poncet analyse how these changed international circumstances began to affect monopoly capital in France which was driven to formulate new locational strategies. The result was to throw an increasing number of French regions into 'active crisis'. Subsequent State intervention to manage these new regional crises has only made conditions worse.

Since 1974, the international recession has 'overlain' and in a sense 'standardised' pre-existing regional crises. However, it is Damette and Poncet's contention that precisely because there is a 'global crisis', State Monopoly Capitalism has begun to lose control at a regional level. They conclude that 'serious cracks have already appeared; others are on the way.'

This analysis was first published before the full regional effects of the international recession had begun to be expressed. Nevertheless, their conclusions have been amply confirmed by subsequent events in France, some of which are discussed in Chapter 2. This chapter also analyses the contradictory character of the relationships between accumulation imperatives and regional problems but goes beyond Damette and Poncet's account in considering examples of political movements associated with 'unresolved' regional problems.

According to the interpretation put forward in Chapter 2, regional problems are a permanent and necessary feature of accumulation in late capitalism. Yet, paradoxically, regional problems also threaten to disrupt accumulation. In late capitalism State intervention in regional problems seeks to resolve this contradiction. However, in most European countries the deepening entanglement of the State in regional problems has, in fact, coincided with their deterioration and has often only served to amplify and generalise regional crisis tendencies.

The failures of State interventions in regional problems have given rise to opportunities for the establishment and growth of new nationalist and regionalist movements which have begun to precipitate acute disruption of 'normal' political activity in several European countries. This has still further eroded the effectiveness of State interventions.

Chapter 2 suggests that since the onset of the international recession, regional crisis tendencies have been considerably strengthened and in some cases have served to trigger the formation of much wider crises. It is concluded that specifically regional paths of crisis formation are likely to become even more important in the future and that this is bound seriously to threaten the coherence of late capitalism in at least some of the most advanced countries in Europe.[8]

Theoretical Issues

Accumulation Imperatives and the Production and Reproduction of Regional Labour Reserves

In Chapter 4 Damette argues that under the pressure of international competition, monopoly capital is driven to discover new locational strategies which will permit 'surplus profits' to be realised. As Lipietz points out in Chapter 3, the advantages to capital of decentralising the most labour-intensive parts of the production process to cheap labour regions can be considerable. Hence there are extremely strong imperatives impelling the search for and industrialisation of regional labour reserves.

However, the exploitation of these reserves may quickly disrupt the very conditions that made these regions initially so attractive to monopoly capital. Branch circuit industrialisation, as Lipietz suggests, may actually reinforce 'extraverted accumulation' and the dissolution of existing social conditions in labour reserve regions. However, because branch circuit industrialisation depends on large-scale regional modernisation programmes, State intervention may actually increase the disruption of existing social conditions and settlement structure. To avoid this outcome other, non-disruptive forms of industrialisation have also evolved, although none are free from contradictions. In Italy, for example, 'diffuse industrialisation' has been an extremely important means of crisis postponement.

In 1962-3, there was a particularly fierce crisis in North-West Italy[9] brought about by a round of wage demands and strikes which were a response to heavy local inflation caused by massive housing and infrastructure shortages. The crisis was only resolved when employers agreed to make large wage increases. This, however, immediately threatened the international competitiveness of all sectors of the Italian economy with capacity concentrated in the North-West.

Some companies dealt with these circumstances by rapidly altering prevailing technologies and product lines through large-scale new investment. Others were unable to follow this strategy and went out of business. In either case, labour-intensive products and activities contracted and in so doing left a gap in the international market which was increasingly filled by existing or newly established small and medium-sized firms located in the Central and North-Eastern regions in Italy.[10] This process occurred spontaneously, owing little to State intervention.

The small firms in these regions proved capable of organising local labour reserves in a way which did not disturb the prevailing social conditions or settlement structure. Most workers in the new industries retained ties with agricultural activities and hence were not subject to the complete proletarianisation experienced by Southern migrants to the North-West in the 1950s. This meant that unionisation was very much weaker. For these reasons, wage costs could be considerably reduced and their subsequent growth very tightly restricted.

This form of 'diffuse' industrialisation allowed the Italian economy to be restructured so that although traditional labour-intensive production contracted in the North-West, new capacity was established in the Central and North-Eastern regions which was internationally competitive. Hence labour-intensive products continued to account for a high proportion of Italian manufactured exports after 1963.

Diffuse industrialisation has meant, however, that the economies of the North-Eastern and Central regions have become increasingly specialised in labour-intensive production. The international competitiveness of these regional economies relies almost entirely on the preservation of social conditions conducive to wage reductions and wage cost control. Hence the economies of the North-Eastern and Central regions now occupy a peculiarly vulnerable position in the international division of labour. Precisely because of the success of diffuse industrialisation, the possibilities of continual productivity gains and technical progress have been systematically eliminated in the two regions.

Both branch circuit and diffuse industrialisation are responses to the search for ways of exploiting regional labour reserves, but neither process is problem-free. Branch circuit industrialisation often disrupts labour reserves, thereby destroying the possibility of continued cheap labour. Diffuse industrialisation leads to blocked regional development. Yet without an expanding supply of regional labour reserves, accumulation in general is threatened. Moreover, hitherto there has been no method open to capital to allow for the *planned production* of regional labour reserves.

This is why new and more sophisticated forms of State intervention in regional problems have begun to emerge, which aim actually to produce, as well as to manage and control, regional labour reserves and systems of inter-regional migration. With the break-up of strongly unionised industries, under the pressures of the international recession, non-unionised labour reserves are being established in depressed areas and often this is the purpose of State intervention as well as an inadvertent consequence of de-industrialisation.[11] However, even these new forms of intervention may merely result in the 'institutionalisation of chaos'.[12]

The Role of the State in Regional Problems

Evidently, accumulation imperatives make it necessary for new inter-
regional divisions of labour to be established. In Alain Lipietz's view,
the State is 'assigned' the role of co-ordinating this process. Where the
requirements of restructuring come into conflict with 'inherited space'
and local interests, the State is called upon to organise interventions to
impose the 'logic' of monopoly capital. Damette adds to this
interpretation by suggesting that although State intervention clearly
supports the interests of monopoly capital, there is an inherent
instability in this arrangement. Because capital has now become
hypermobile, State interventions increasingly encounter or engender
chaos.

Other contributions also focus upon the 'problem-proneness' of
State interventions in regional problems. Although interventions are
still said to arise as a response to accumulation imperatives, it is
emphasised that the State may not necessarily have the capacity to
comply with these imperatives. This proposition has arisen partly due
to theoretical analysis originating in wider debates on the nature of
the State in late capitalism.[13] It is also supported by a number of case
studies which have begun to show that regional problems have often
deteriorated as a consequence of State interventions apparently
intended to secure their resolution.[14] Other studies have suggested
that the disappearance of regional problems may simply mean that crisis
tendencies have been displaced elsewhere. Increased public expenditures in depressed regions may, for example, temporarily stimulate
economic activity, but only at the expense of a 'hidden' rise in State
debt encumbrance which, in turn, adds to fiscal crisis tendencies and
inflationary pressures.

These interpretations do not deny that specific State interventions in
regional problems can be highly effective. Nevertheless, it is the limits
to State power and control and the aggregate irrationality of the
relationships between accumulation imperatives and the State which are
stressed. The State is no longer represented as being necessarily capable
of performing all the 'co-ordinating' and 'steering' roles required to
sustain accumulation. Indeed, in Damette's view State Monopoly
Capitalism has 'begun to lose control', a process which is most clearly
expressed at a regional level.

Regional Problems and Crisis Formation

Chapter 2 concludes that unresolved regional problems may be transformed into local social crises and, in turn, trigger the formation of much

wider crises. Yet since the onset of the international recession, it is becoming less feasible for State intervention to contain and manage regional problems and regional crises. This is not only because there are major pressures to curtail State expenditure and secure 'balanced budgets',[15] but also because State interventions are increasingly the proximate causes of regional problems. These interventions cannot be abandoned without endangering accumulation in general.

In these circumstances, the hold of conventional politics has been weakened, sometimes to the point where the 'repressive' role of the State has to be openly activated to contain social disorder and regional breakdown. Yet where this has had to occur, in Northern Ireland since 1969 and in Lorraine since the start of 1979, events have shown that this form of State intervention too has definite limits, is inherently problem-prone and, in fact, is likely greatly to worsen the initial problem.[16]

Because specifically regional paths to general crisis formation are likely to become even more important in the future, analysis of the nature of the new regionalist and nationalist political movements emerging in Europe will become increasingly important. It is already evident that there are no rules that will guarantee that these movements will be progressive or that their effects on conventional political life will be progressive.[17]

One scenario is that nationalist and regionalist movements will continue to multiply and expand in response to worsening regional problems, thereby increasingly disrupting conventional politics and further curbing the effectiveness of State interventions in regional problems but that few, if any, will gain power.[18] In this scenario the political landscape of Europe will be fragmented under the overwhelming pressures of the international recession and the consequent strengthening of regional crisis tendencies. This will lead to the break-up of the EEC.

Another scenario is that some of the new nationalist movements might actually win a good deal of autonomy and will do so on the basis of socialist programmes. This is a possibility in Wallonia, in the Saar-Luxemburg-Lorraine area and also in Scotland.[19] A third scenario is that the growth of radical politics in depressed regions will provide a basis for the formation of entirely new coalitions within the EEC.

The continuation of the international recession will certainly result in the emergence of many more regional problems in Europe and create conditions for the sudden eruption of regional crises which, in turn, may trigger general social crises. It is in this context that regional theory will be further elaborated in the eighties as a guide to action as well as a means of interpretation.

Notes

1. G. Myrdal, *Economic Theory and Underdeveloped Regions* (Methuen, London, 1957). For a recent version of Myrdal's theses see S. Holland, *Capital Versus the Regions* (Macmillan, London, 1976).

2. An important initial influence was the growth of radical theory concerned with development and underdevelopment on a world scale. See, for example, A.G. Frank, *Capitalism and Underdevelopment in Latin America* (Penguin, Harmondsworth, 1969). The reformulation of regional theory in Third World countries was also important. See, for instance, M. Santos, *L'Espace Partagé* (Th. Génin, Paris, 1975) and D. Slater 'Underdevelopment and Spatial Inequality', *Progress in Planning*, vol. 4, no. 2 (1975).

3. The term 'mode of production' refers to a distinctive set of technological and social relationships, usually delimited historically. On this basis capitalist and feudal modes of production are, for example, commonly distinguished.

4. See, for example, E. Mandel, *Late Capitalism* (New Left Books, London, 1975), pp. 310-42.

5. Graziani's findings concerning the industrialisation of the Italian Mezzogiorno after 1963 certainly support this hypothesis. See A. Graziani *et al.*, *Investimenti autonomi e investimenti indotti nell' economia del Mezzogiorno* (University of Naples, Naples, 1977).

6. The 'law of value' results from the competitive allocation of surplus value between different capitals through the exchange of commodities. Under non-competitive conditions, temporary departures from the average rate of profit can become permanent, making some forms of investment, regardless of their importance to accumulation in general, highly unattractive to private capital.

7. See Chapter 7.

8. This conclusion is also implicit in Damette's work. As well as Chapters 4 and 5, see the other references to Damette listed in Chapter 7.

9. Comprising Piemonte, Valle d'Aosta, Liguria and Lombardia.

10. The Central region comprises Toscana, Umbria, Marche and Lazio. The North-Eastern region is made up of Trentino-Alto Adige, Veneto, Friuli-Venezia-Giulia and Emilia Romagna.

11. See Chapter 2.

12. See, for example, Damette's comments in Chapter 4.

13. See Chapter 7.

14. Two of the most detailed empirical accounts to date are Graziani's *Investimenti autonomi* and J. Carney and R. Hudson, *State Regional Policies and Uneven Development: the Case of the North East* (Centre for Environmental Studies, London, 1979).

15. Accelerating inflation gives rise to these pressures. For a fuller analysis, see E. Mandel, *The Second Slump* (New Left Books, London, 1978), pp. 90-101.

16. On Northern Ireland see M. Farrell, *Northern Ireland: the Orange State* (Pluto Press, London, 1976), especially pp. 257-321.

17. A point emphasised by Tom Nairn in his seminal book, *The Break-Up of Britain* (New Left Books, London, 1977). Nairn's views on this and many other points are strongly challenged in Eric Hobsbawm's review, 'Some Reflections on "The Break-up of Britain" ', *New Left Review*, no. 105 (1977), pp. 3-23.

18. We are indebted to Tom Nairn for this scenario – eds.

19. The heavy defeat of the SNP in the 1979 general election in Britain may,

paradoxically, have brought the prospect nearer. As explained in Tom Nairn's article, 'The Clans that will Live to Regroup', *Guardian* (21 May 1979), the SNP's defeat was implicit in the very nature of its earlier successes, 'which relied far too heavily upon a cloudy, unradical brand of nationalism – tweedy, classless modernisation – without tears'. Since this ideology has been found to be incapable of mobilising majority support in conditions of increasing economic adversity, nationalist politics may be forced into much more radical channels, a point also made in Chapter 2.

2 REGIONS IN CRISIS: ACCUMULATION, REGIONAL PROBLEMS AND CRISIS FORMATION

John Carney

Introduction

This chapter explores the relationships between accumulation imperatives, regional problems and crisis formation using illustrations from
countries and regions within Europe. It is argued that regional problems
provide necessary pre-conditions for capital accumulation or are
inescapable consequences of it. As such, regional problems are a permanent and necessary feature of late capitalism. However, although
essential to accumulation, regional problems may also give rise to
circumstances which threaten accumulation. Regional problems present
opportunities for the growth of regionalist and nationalist political
movements which can bring about the destabilisation of 'normal'
political life, hence adding to the uncertainties surrounding State interventions without which continued accumulation would be endangered.

Capital Accumulation

General Features of Accumulation

In the capitalist mode of production, the accumulation of capital arises
from the production of commodities and since in this mode of production the means of production along with labour power are commodities, capital accumulation may be analysed in terms of exchange
values.[1] This first involves the identification of the component parts of
capital. To do so it is necessary to distinguish between: (1) capital
advanced in a production period and (2) surplus value which is created
through production, is appropriated and then realised on the successful
sale of the commodities produced.

The capital advanced during a production period may be further
divided into: (1) variable capital and (2) constant capital. Variable
capital is the sum of the exchange values of the commodities that enter
into the reproduction of labour power. It is the exchange value equivalent of the wage bill. Constant capital is the sum expended on circulating and fixed capital. The former comprises fuel and raw materials,
the latter, buildings, machinery and the like.

Surplus value, created through production, is the difference between the exchange value of total output during a production period and the sum of variable and constant capital advanced in this period. The difference arises as a result of the exchange between the owners of the means of production as opposed to the owners of labour power in which the value that will be created by applying labour to commodities is ignored. This value is taken by the owners of the means of production as their reward.

Using these concepts, accumulation can be defined. It is the central process of the capitalist mode of production; a process which operates blindly from one production period to another. Surplus value realised in one production period and not used for consumption may be laid out in a subsequent period, in a certain proportion, to hire more workers, to purchase additional fuel, raw materials, machinery and buildings. The consequent expenditure is expressed as overall and specific rates of investment within a general accumulation process.

One of the principal determinants of rates of investment and hence the pace of accumulation is the rate of profit. From the previous definitions, this may be identified as a relationship between surplus value and the sum of variable and constant capital advanced in a production period. Hence a rise in the value of labour power would, by increasing outlays on variable capital, tend to reduce the rate of profit and hence disturb accumulation. Likewise a rise in the value of items of constant capital would adversely affect profitability and accumulation, as would a fall in the mass of realised surplus value. Conversely, the cheapening of variable and constant capital and an expansion in the mass of realised surplus value would all tend to accelerate the pace and scale of accumulation.

For a single unit of capital it is not enough to maintain a constant rate of profit over several production periods. Other units of capital may be expanding at a faster pace and enjoying a higher rate of profit. Hence every unit of capital is affected by a strong imperative to seek out above-average profits. Therefore, within the accumulation process, units of capital must seek to expand or else risk disappearance and clearly this expansion must be linked to the pursuit of a higher rate of profit as well as the search for a greater mass of profits.

The double imperative of expansion and profitability as it operates at the level of a single unit of capital does not, however, result in a smooth accumulation of 'capital in general'. A well known illustration of this is investment by a single unit of capital in fixed capital so as to increase labour productivity and thus allow the production and appropriation of excess profits. Unless the rise in productivity is substantial, the general introduction of this investment has the effect of restoring a uniform but lower rate of profit for capital as a whole. Nor are either of the standard responses to this tendency — an increase in production or a reduction in wages — problem-free. The aggregate effect of the former is to expand production beyond the ability of the market to absorb the additional output while the latter involves the contraction of the market. While either of these solutions is rational for the individual capitalist, the aggregate effect of both is that not all the surplus value embodied in commodities can be realised. As a consequence, profitability declines and accumulation is threatened. Hence accumulation, the main driving force of the capitalist mode of production, follows an inherently 'crisis-ridden' course with 'successive phases of recession, upswing, boom, overheating, crash and depression'.[2] This was true of liberal capitalism and remains true in late capitalism.

In liberal capitalism, interruptions of accumulation by periodic crises were immediately transformed into social crises, a process of crisis formation that appeared to have the character of a 'natural event' and one which could not be subject to societal regulation. One of the main characteristics of late capitalism is that State intervention provides a means of arresting a recession before it can take on a massively cumulative force, but this does not imply that crisis-free accumulation will result. Economic crisis tendencies in late capitalism may be repressed by State interventions but this may be achieved only at the expense of generating new forms of crisis.

Despite the crisis-ridden character of accumulation, long-period expansion in output and capacity within a capitalist economy may occur if the necessary pre-conditions are present. Yet generally these are so stringent that the possibility of long-run growth tendencies in a capitalist economy is strictly limited and long-run growth paths appear to be seriously and inherently unstable.[3]

In the formation and resolution of accumulation crises 'automatic' recovery tendencies operate so that an upturn occurs due to the existence of conditions created by a recession.[4] However, there is no guarantee that recovery will involve a return to the levels of capacity utilisation previously experienced. Nor is there any guarantee that full employment will be reached, since the existence of a large reserve of labour is an essential condition for profitable accumulation, even though this tends to restrict the growth of the market for consumer goods. State intervention to assist the 'automatic' process of recovery is also necessary, although this does not guarantee that a long-run growth path can be rediscovered and maintained. As well as allowing the actual onset of a recession to be controlled, State intervention aims to steer and transform the economy so as to avoid crises. This takes the form of short-term 'demand management' measures, but also involves long-term investment programmes aimed at promoting economic 'restructuring' without which accumulation would be endangered.[5]

In a crisis, the value of each component part of capital is severely reduced as a means of eventually restoring pre-conditions for a new burst of accumulation. Thus, at all times, but especially at crisis points, units of capital and 'capital in general' are seeking to discover or reproduce conditions that will permit the component parts of capital to be cheapened. This 'blind' process is intimately connected with the origins and reproduction of what are conventionally called 'regional problems'.

Variable Capital

From the foregoing remarks, it can be seen that a reduction in the value of labour power would contribute to a rise in the rate of profit and could, in specific circumstances, help to resolve an accumulation crisis, hence establishing conditions that would allow renewed accumulation to occur. Thus there is a specific imperative, arising from the accumulation process, for arrangements to be evolved whereby labour power may be reduced in value. This imperative arises at the level of units of capital and holds for capital in general. It will operate throughout the industrial cycle but is likely to be particularly strong at a crisis point.

A necessary condition for the establishment and early expansion of the capitalist mode of production was the destruction of the pre-capitalist countryside. This affected variable capital in two main ways. First, it allowed the expansion of an urban labour force, while maintaining the countryside as an area where an industrial reserve army could be reproduced. Second, it allowed the value of foodstuffs and other consumption goods to be reduced, in turn permitting reductions in the value of labour power. Yet the invasion of rural areas by capital was a very partial process and in many regions of Western Europe pre-capitalist relations of production in agriculture remained predominant up to 1939. Even rural areas where capitalist agriculture was dominant were largely depressed at this time.

These areas were characterised by low productivity, high unemployment and underemployment, low consumer expenditure and very little social provision. Often transportation, electricity and other infrastructure were non-existent or of very limited capacity. After 1945 such areas presented what appeared to be the most serious regional problems. Because agricultural productivity was so low and due to wartime dislocations, there was a huge shortage of food in Europe which the backward agricultural sector could not hope to meet. At the same time these areas were marked by mass poverty and hence provided barriers to the expansion of the domestic market within most European economies.[6]

The transformation of depressed rural areas in Europe was, therefore, a crucial pre-condition for rapid accumulation. In many of these areas capitalist methods were applied for the first time to the rural economy. In part, this was the result of the post-war food scarcity which led to the formation of above-average rates of profit in agriculture and, in turn, to an unprecedented inrush of capital into agriculture. The 'industrialisation' of agriculture in formerly depressed regions was also important as a way of expanding the market for some of the leading new industries in late capitalism, such as chemicals and motor vehicle production. The transformation of depressed rural areas also made it possible for a large proportion of the unemployed and underemployed labour forces in these areas to be incorporated through migration systems into urban labour forces in the main centres of accumulation in Europe.

The migrations caused by the war served to meet initial labour demands in the reconstruction of European economies but thereafter, large-scale migration from depressed rural areas to the principal centres of accumulation and labour demand was crucial in maintaining conditions necessary for continued expansion. The scale of accumulation was allowed to expand for several years without resulting in rising wage costs through the continued growth in the volume of inter-regional migration. However, the pace of acceleration of accumulation and hence of labour demand soon began to outrun even the possibilities offered by this system. General conditions of full employment arose in the centres of accumulation and became a serious threat to profitability and hence to further accumulation. With full employment it began to be possible for wages to be driven up, wage demands being partly a response to inflationary tendencies arising through infrastructure shortages. In these circumstances, to avoid a crisis in accumulation, additional new manpower and investment planning arrangements had to be evolved.

The industrialisation of the depressed rural areas in Europe which had previously simply acted as labour reserves began to occur. In some cases this was an 'unplanned' process which did not disturb existing social relationships in the rural areas concerned.[7] Elsewhere, State interventions were used to co-ordinate the 'planned' industrialisation of backward rural areas;[8] to establish the necessary industrial infrastructure and often to advance the required capital through State banks and holding companies. At the same time, capital in agriculture was deliberately reorganised through State intervention along with agricultural infrastructure. Often this had the effect of accelerating the expulsion of labour from agriculture and associated small-scale manufacturing activities.[9] This labour was then brought into the existing inter-regional labour migration systems.

However, a large number of additional sources of migrant labour were also produced by a new and different strategy whereby hitherto stagnant countries, often colonies or former colonies of European states, were drawn into the accumulation process. Hence international systems of migrant labour began to be established, the advantages of which were considerable. No outlays were required initially to produce the labourers. The labour force could be tightly controlled and carefully selected by employers and the State in the receiving countries and unionisation made impossible. Such migrant labour could be easily laid off and repatriated at the first sign of a recession and re-imported as required to brake wage inflation. Thus the 'discovery' and establishment of an international migrant labour system seemed to provide a major means of crisis avoidance.[10]

Another investment strategy which sought to overcome labour shortages and reduce wage costs was also evolved. This was to 'relocate' manufacturing capacity in backward countries, through international direct investment, a strategy only possible because of the advanced character of the international concentration and centralisation of capital in the form of multinational manufacturing companies.

The intention of these strategies was that individual units of capital and capital in general would be able to reduce outlays on variable capital and to avoid labour shortages and hence the possible disruption of accumulation due to reduced profitability caused by wage inflation and the enhanced working-class combativity which often accompanies full employment. To be successful, these strategies had to preserve the initial conditions found in depressed rural regions and countries drawn into the accumulation process; conditions that involved 'unlimited labour forever'. Yet direct investment in manufacturing capacity, the break-up of agriculture and the establishment and expansion of migrant labour systems all threaten to have profoundly disruptive effects and to create crises in the economic and social life of the backward countries and regions concerned.

Such disruption would undermine the very conditions which first made the depressed rural economies 'attractive' to capital. Only in a few cases has it proved possible for there to be a 'diffuse' industrialisation of a formerly depressed rural area, whereby the initial conditions have been preserved in the course of industrialisation. Mostly, the economies of these areas have progressively disintegrated under the effects of agricultural modernisation, migrant labour and State intervention.

Yet a reserve of these areas is a necessary pre-condition for continued accumulation and crisis avoidance. Thus the search for new areas with conditions of 'unlimited labour forever' has become a permanent feature of late capitalism. This search has not, however, merely been confined to rural areas. State intervention in coalfield and industrial areas, in certain circumstances, can actually produce new concentrations of surplus labour and thus, to an extent, add to the capacity of the reserve of areas characterised by conditions of 'unlimited labour forever'.

Circulating Constant Capital

The rate of profit can be raised if the value of constant capital is reduced. Conversely, a rise in the value of constant capital may seriously threaten profitability and hence accumulation. Thus there are strong pressures to reduce the values of commodities that go to make up this component part of capital.

Circulating constant capital comprises fuels and the raw materials of production. In all the leading European economies after 1945, fuel and raw materials shortages threatened seriously to retard accumulation. In response, two strategies were pursued and each involved State-initiated 'co-ordinating activities'.

In 1945 the leading European economies were dependent on a single fuel: coal. To sustain rapid general accumulation it was necessary to carry out huge new investment programmes to expand coal-mining capacity. This could have been undertaken by allowing coal prices to rise to a level that permitted an above-average rate of profit in coal-mining which would have made this sector attractive for new investment. However, a sharp rise in coal prices would have reduced profitability and hence retarded growth in all other sectors. An alternative policy was for the rate of investment in coal-mining to be divorced from the rate of profit through State intervention. This policy would ensure that adequate new investment took place only at the expense of increasing State indebtedness. Nevertheless, the policy had the advantage of 'guaranteeing' a vital pre-condition for general accumulation in all other sectors.

The second strategy was to 'convert' the fuel-supply system in Europe so that several sources and kinds of fuel could be used rather than a single fuel. In effect, the aim was to replace coal with cheaper fuels. However, this policy also required large amounts of new investment, especially in infrastructure provision, much of which appeared to be unprofitable and again required heavy State financial and co-ordinating intervention. Oil and natural gas consumption in Europe expanded very rapidly after the mid-fifties. This would not have been possible if capital had not already been organised in the form of multi-national companies. Nor would it have occurred without considerable State intervention to ensure that the international trade in oil was secure as well as to ensure that capacity existed to refine and distribute output.

These two fuel strategies were, clearly, contradictory. It was necessary to modernise the coal industry immediately to make early post-war reconstruction possible. However, the timing of the implementation of the switch to multi-fuel economies was much less certain. When large amounts of cheap oil and natural gas became available on the international market, this had a 'sudden' and 'unanticipated' effect on the coal industry in Europe. Much of the new investment in the coal industry was rendered uncompetitive by the sharp fall in fuel prices and there was a rapid contraction of the market share of the coal industry in the international energy market. This 'sudden' conversion towards cheap fuel provided an essential stimulus to long-period accumulation. However, it simultaneously gave rise to serious new regional problems. From being areas with conditions of full employment and heavy investment in fixed capital, the economies of many coalfield areas in Europe began to disintegrate as a result of the success of the cheap fuel policies essential to general accumulation.

New programmes of State intervention were hastily devised to deal with the regional consequences of cheap fuel policies. The contraction of employment in coalfield areas seemed to present an opportunity to alleviate labour shortages. Indeed coalfield contraction was often speeded up through State intervention so that manpower could be more quickly 'released' to meet labour shortages in other sectors and regions. Thus the newly produced regional problem created fresh labour reserves within domestic economies where the effects of full employment were beginning to brake accumulation. However, to take advantage of these new labour reserves, considerable infrastructure investment was required to permit the establishment of new manufacturing capacity. This was a particularly difficult process to co-ordinate since the pace of decline of coal-mining was not under State control but rather reflected imperatives in the international market for fuel. As a result, in most coalfield areas, only a very partial re-industrialisation was achieved which left these new problem regions with permanently higher levels of unemployment. In this way the transformation of the coalfield areas made a major contribution to the reconstitution of labour reserves within the domestic economies of most of the main European countries. Thus the reproduction of this kind of regional problem became a permanent feature of late capitalism.

Raw materials also make up an important part of circulating constant capital. To sustain rapid accumulation in Europe it was necessary to discover huge new sources of raw materials and to invent entirely new ones. The response was an unprecedented international search for raw materials led by multinational companies and co-ordinated by State interventions, combined with a massive expansion in research and development expenditure to discover new raw materials. This had the effect of producing numerous new regions which have only a single role in the international division of labour and of leading to the establishment of a vast amount of capacity and production complexes to produce the new artificial raw materials.

The location of new raw materials production complexes, because of their scale of operation and environmental impacts, thus, in turn, became a new regional problem. The expenses incurred in the establishment of such complexes and the length of time involved in producing the necessary infrastructure capacity quickly made their production too expensive even for the largest multinational companies. Yet, at the same time, the expansion of capital in general was vitally dependent on the new raw materials. The complexes also provided essential markets for many important branches of engineering. Hence there were extremely strong imperatives directed at involving the State in the provision of the necessary but unprofitable items of infrastructure required to establish the complexes. It was also necessary for there to be an extremely sophisticated form of long-run infrastructure and land-use planning in the complexes to ensure their orderly growth.

Initially, State intervention in fuel production, coalfield reconversion and raw materials production appeared to be successful. It seemed to be leading to the elimination of major barriers to sustained accumulation. Yet the huge increase in State involvement in the production of fuels and raw materials gave rise to unprecedented financial burdens and, moreover, severely tested the co-ordinating capacity of the State. In some cases, a form of intervention capable of managing huge infra-structure investment and conversion was achieved, notably in the Netherlands and West Germany.[11] In other cases, such as the involve-ment of the British State in coalfield industrialisation[12] and of the Italian State in underwriting the establishment of petrochemical com-plexes,[13] these new demands exposed a condition of 'structural incom-petence'.

Fixed Constant Capital

The value of fixed capital is established by the conditions and impera-tives obtaining in the production goods industries. A reduction in the value of fixed capital, that is plant, machinery and buildings, will lead to a rise in the rate of profit and hence will encourage accumulation. Moreover, because technical progress resulting from research and development activity is introduced into an economy through improve-ments in equipment, the installation of new machinery can present opportunities for the realisation of excess profits. There is thus a strong and continual imperative to reduce the value of fixed capital and to introduce new equipment.

Yet although the introduction of new machinery is vitally necessary for accumulation in general, it can have complicated side-effects which arise as a result of technical obsolescence. Existing fixed capital is rendered obsolete as a consequence of general tendencies towards the reduction in value of fixed capital. This applies to fixed capital in all sectors, including the production goods industries.

Advances in technique in the production of machinery may also be incorporated into the production of consumption goods. Clearly, a reduction in the value of consumption goods (including housing) would lead to a reduction in the value of labour power, hence to an increase in the general rate of profit. This reduction could arise through investment in new machinery. There is thus a general imperative to replace less with more productive arrangements in consumption goods production. Moreover, in a world market for such goods there are considerable opportunities for individual units of capital to make excess profits through the introduction of new techniques of production. Hence, there are also both general and specific pressures for an increase in the pace of obsolescence in consumption goods production.

If the pace of technical change accelerates, there is, then, the possi-bility that a considerable part of the world capacity in certain branches of production will have to be scrapped because it has been rendered obsolete. If this does not happen, general accumulation is retarded. If it does, many units of capital are ruined. Obsolescence may be combined with disinvestment from units of capital rendered unprofitable by technical progress. Unprofitability for a unit of capital, or indeed for a branch of production, may, of course, occur for other reasons, such as over-production, and disinvestment may occur as a result of amalgamation and closure policies, that is the centralisation and concentration of capital. State intervention may also hasten the closure of obsolete and unprofitable branches of production. Such intervention may have the intention of releasing labour power for other activities or of making the remaining part of an industry more profitable.

In late capitalism, the production of the items of fixed capital is organised on an international scale. One of the difficulties for State intervention seeking to 'modernise' production goods manufacture is that the international concentration of manufacturing capacity often involves the complete disappearance of branches of production from national economies. Thus, State interventions to modernise national manufacturing capacity can be continuously thrown into disarray because technical progress and consequent technological obsolescence arise internationally, outside the control of single nation-states. Moreover, technical progress is very closely connected with an acceleration in the international concentration of capital. This too undermines the co-ordinating power of nation-states. Ironically, State interventions to modernise declining industrial regions have often followed policies of 'attracting' foreign capital in order to replace obsolete production with industries with more advanced methods of production.

Under free-trade arrangements, it is not necessarily possible for the State in a single country to control de-industrialisation. Nor are there necessarily 'automatic' adjustments so that de-industrialisation could be expected to be 'self-regulating'. Hence it is possible that regions within the international economy could be entirely de-industrialised as a *necessary* consequence of rearrangements in the international division of labour which are vital to the survival and further expansion of individual units of capital.

In Europe, since the late fifties, de-industrialisation has affected the British economy most severely, although the Netherlands and Belgium have also experienced some contraction in manufacturing capacity and employment. The first signs of technological obsolescence, falling competitiveness and de-industrialisation began to become apparent in Britain at the end of the fifties and were immediately expressed as 'regional problems' in Northern Ireland, Lancashire, Scotland and

North-East England.

In each case, similar 'solutions' were advanced. The 'co-ordinating' power of the State would be used to protect declining industries, to reduce capacity and restore international competitiveness. In addition, comprehensive regional modernisation programmes were proposed which aimed to provide the necessary infrastructural pre-conditions for renewed accumulation in these worn-out industrial regions as quickly as possible. These programmes were intended to act through a rapid and steep rise in public expenditure which would be maintained until 'self-sustaining' growth could be re-established, after which State expenditures would be reduced again.

In fact, in the sixties, the pace of industrial contraction accelerated; further regional concentrations of obsolete capacity emerged at the same time as an unprecedented expansion in State expenditures on regional modernisation. Neither sectoral nor regional policies resulted in lasting gains in competitiveness or arrested de-industrialisation in the peripheral regions. Even worse, after 1966, de-industrialisation began to affect the formerly most prosperous regions in the national economy, namely the South-East and the Midlands. In fact, the rates of reduction of manufacturing employment and capacity in these regions soon outstripped those continuing to be experienced in the depressed industrial regions.[14] As a consequence, State expenditures had to be hugely increased in order to offset the decline in effective demand for labour in the South and the Midlands that would otherwise have resulted from de-industrialisation. In turn, this made it more difficult for the continuing industrial decline in the peripheral regions to be arrested and also greatly contributed to the expansion of State debt encumbrance and the strength of fiscal crisis tendencies in the British economy.

Clearly, in the British case, despite a huge increase in State intervention intended to avoid de-industrialisation, manufacturing decline was not arrested. It was possible to avoid some of the labour-market consequences by expanding public expenditure in regions worst affected by industrial decline, but this did not restore competitiveness, nor did it result in the absorption of redundant labour from obsolete manufacturing into new branches of manufacturing. Rather, in all the regions affected by this process, redundant labour was drawn into mainly low-paid service sector activities, a result which was entirely unanticipated, or added to permanent unemployment. The regional problems resulting from industrial decline in Britain thus deteriorated at the same time as unprecedented expansion of State intervention designed to solve them.

This was because the international accumulation imperatives in operation were so strong as to be beyond the capacity of the 'co-ordinating' power of the British State. Yet at an international level, the restructuring involved was vitally necessary to continued accumulation in other leading capitalist economies and to the continued expansion of multinational capital.

Accumulation Imperatives and Regional Problems

Using this interpretation, regional problems as conventionally defined are seen as arising as necessary concomitants of capital accumulation. For this reason, regional problems have become a permanent feature of late capitalism. In a period of rapid accumulation, new regional problems are produced in order to provide pre-conditions for accelerated accumulation and as the consequence of rapid growth in areas where accumulation is concentrated.[15] In a period of recession, in order to arrest the fall in the rate of profit and to reconstitute a reserve army of labour, additional new regional problems are produced through the devalorisation of capital required to re-establish pre-conditions for renewed accumulation.

Yet although the production of regional problems is, therefore, inescapably linked to accumulation, there is no guarantee that the continual production of regional problems will be automatically self-regulating. It is possible for regional problems to get out of control and turn into *regional crises*. Regional crisis tendencies are therefore produced as part of the process of accumulation and will be present even in a period of generally 'successful' accumulation. In a period of general recession, when even the principal centres of accumulation may be affected, regional crises will be even more likely to erupt.

Paradoxically, although formed as a necessary consequence of accumulation imperatives, regional problems and regional crisis tendencies constitute a serious threat to accumulation. Depressed agricultural, coalfield and industrial regions still present formidable barriers to the expansion of the domestic market in the EEC. Over-accumulation in the main centres of accumulation threatens to trigger explosive inflation. Nevertheless, the continued reproduction and indeed worsening of these regional problems is a necessary condition of accelerated accumulation. For this reason, State crisis management and crisis-avoidance machinery has come to be heavily involved in controlling the regional consequences of accumulation imperatives, so that, especially in depressed areas, the concentration of high levels of permanent unemployment and of economic dislocation do not spill over into social crisis.

However, there are very severe limits on the ability of the State to manage the regional consequences of accumulation imperatives. Partly this is because of the internationalisation of production which erodes the capacity of single nation-states to implement policies to promote expansion in depressed regions. It is also due to the inherently ineffectual character of the State in dealing with the suddenness with which new regional problems can emerge, as a result, for instance, of changes in production technology which swiftly render a large amount of existing capacity in the international economy obsolete. The ability of the State to control the regional effects of accumulation imperatives also depends on the extent to which existing social and cultural conditions in depressed regions provide opportunities for the generalisation of economic crisis tendencies so that these become transformed into a set of social demands which may even call into question the legitimacy of the State. Often in depressed areas the existing social structure provides considerable opportunities for capital. This seems to have been the case, for instance, in North-Eastern and Central Italy in 1962 and 1963.[16]

Nevertheless, the continual production of regional problems in combination with specific social and cultural inheritances has given rise to regionalist and nationalist political movements, some of which have threatened to disrupt accumulation and conventional political life. Indeed, such movements along with regional problems, have become strongly established in several advanced European countries.

Regions in Crisis and Crisis Formation

The contention that the crisis-proneness of accumulation and of State interventions in regional problems have increasingly provided opportunities for the growth of political movements in depressed regions is illustrated here by reference to three cases. The first concerns uneven regional development in Belgium and the rise of demands for the break-up of the Belgian State. The second deals with the recent history of nationalism in Scotland which has seemed to threaten the break-up of the British State. The final case refers to events during early 1979 in Lorraine and Nord-Pas-de-Calais in France.

Uneven Regional Development and Crisis Formation in Belgium

One of the first major post-war regional crises in Europe occurred in Belgium between 1960 and 1961. It was described shortly afterwards by Ernest Mandel, who suggested that the wholly unexpected emerg-

ence at this time of popular nationalism in Wallonia was precipitated by
the relative successes of Flemish nationalism combined with the
beginning of an economic decline in Wallonia.[17]

In the first years after 1945, the Belgian economy was the strongest
in Europe. Industrial capacity was relatively intact compared to that
of other Continental countries, and Antwerp was the only large and
undamaged port on the North Sea. As a consequence, sufficient foreign
exchange was earned to allow imports to be freed from controls very
quickly. In addition, the Belgian Empire reached a peak of development between 1944 and 1955, when profits from the Congo accounted
for one-third of all the dividends of Belgian companies. In these circumstances, the financial groups controlling the economy had little
incentive to initiate major structural changes. This meant that the introduction of 'new industries' such as machine-tools, pharmaceuticals,
synthetic fibres, electronics and consumer durables was severely
retarded. Yet it was precisely these industries which, after 1953, made a
major contribution to expansion in other European economies. As a
consequence, the rate of growth of the Belgian economy between
1954 and 1960 was markedly lower than in West Germany, Italy,
France or the Netherlands.[18] Moreover, the delay in modernising and
diversifying the economy also coincided with increasing industrialisation 'of the countries which provided Belgian industry with its traditional outlets'.[19]

The result was that by the end of the fifties, the Belgian economy
was coming to occupy 'an increasingly marginal position in the world
market'.[20] Belgium was the only country in the EEC to be severely
affected by the 1958 recession which triggered the sequential collapse
of several older industries. Rolling-stock production was the first and
worst affected,[21] even though it had once been crucial to Belgian
export growth. By the end of the fifties, rolling-stock production had
been virtually eliminated. From 1958 onwards, the coal industry in
Wallonia also began to be affected by a fierce process of contraction.
The industry had lost nearly all its former foreign outlets and American
coal had begun to take a large share of the Belgian domestic market.
Within a few years, a third of the capacity of the coal industry was
eliminated through colliery closures.

For most of the fifties, successive Belgian governments denied that
the rapid modernisation of the Belgian economy was necessary.
However, in 1960 a crash programme was proposed made up of a series
of measures designed to stimulate investment in 'new industries' and a
package of fiscal measures and expenditure controls to pay for the

investment subsidies. The government hoped that any hostile response to these measures would be confined to workers directly affected by the proposed reductions in public expenditure. As expected, public employees began a strike on 28 December 1960 but during the following week a spontaneous movement spread throughout Wallonia in support of the public-sector workers. The movement quickly turned into a general strike in the region but only won minority support in Flanders. In subsequent weeks, the State was thus able to confine the strike to Wallonia and eventually defeated it, although most of the deflationary proposals in the government's modernisation programme were dropped and the government subsequently lost a general election.

After the strike, comparisons were drawn in Wallonia 'between the remarkable success of the general strike' there and its 'relative failure in Flanders'. Some elements in the Walloon labour movement concluded that its activities would be condemned to years of stagnation if it 'remained tied to the concept of a unitary Belgium'.[22]

To wait until the majority of Flemish workers achieved a level of politicisation comparable to Wallonia seemed to mean risking the disintegration of trade union and socialist support in the region. This conclusion was drawn from the labour movement's experience of the effects of de-industrialisation on political life in Wallonia. Further economic decline would weaken socialist support and trade union membership still more. There was by no means unanimous agreement within the Walloon labour movement that this analysis or the prescriptions arising from it were correct. However, there was sufficient support for it to permit the establishment of a Walloon Popular Movement which demanded a federal structure for Belgium in the belief that under such a system, the Walloon working class would have a chance to implement 'anti-capitalist' structural reforms, something that had proved impossible under the unitary Belgian State.[23] The Popular Movement did not, however, advocate the break-up of the Belgian State.

The crisis of 1960-1 was, therefore, in the short term 'contained' by virtue of the existence of strong regional differences within Belgium. The preservation, in Flanders, of a weakly industrialised regional economy within what was an internationally advanced economy had given Belgian capital a considerable competitive edge before 1914. In 1961, not only did the existence of a politically conservative labour reserve in Flanders help to arrest the spontaneous growth of the general strike movement, it also provided an essential means of implementing the long overdue modernisation of the Belgian economy.

After 1961, investment in the 'new industries' previously 'missing' from the Belgian economy went ahead very quickly. Compared to the very slow growth in GDP between 1955 and 1960, there was a rapid acceleration in accumulation in Belgium after 1960. Between 1960 and 1965, Belgian GDP grew by 5.3 per cent per annum; from 1964-9 by 4.0 per cent and from 1969-73 by 5.2 per cent. These growth rates were much nearer to the EEC average than previously and were the result of a switch in the regional allocation of industrial investment in Belgium that was engineered through concerted State intervention in modernising the Belgian economy. The system of sectoral and regional investment incentives established in 1959 and 1960 was considerably strengthened during the sixties and it was this system that underwrote the unprecedented industrialisation of the Flanders region after 1960. This process was led by the establishment of petrochemicals production in the Antwerp area and in the Ghent-Terneuzen Canal zone. In 1967, for the first time, *per capita* income in Flanders was greater than in Wallonia where the regional economy grew at rates similar to or below those experienced in the fifties.[24]

The structural problems of the Belgian economy which emerged in the late fifties were, therefore, resolved and a period of rapid accumulation ensued, through the reproduction and expansion of regional imbalances. The new imbalances, in turn, acted upon the existing political and cultural divisions in Belgium. The potentially volatile combination of a sharp reversal in relative prosperity linked to continuing linguistic and cultural antagonisms remained suppressed, however, until the mid-seventies, when a major political crisis developed.

For a time during 1978 it appeared as if an acceptable plan to establish a type of federal state could be devised.[25] This prospect faded in the autumn when the Tindemans coalition resigned. After an inconclusive general election, the break-up of the Belgian State became a serious possibility and there was an apparent structural incapacity to reach agreement on a 'federal solution' of the sort envisaged in 1961 by the Walloon Popular Movement. In Wallonia support was growing for secessionist demands, a process accelerated by the severe impact of the international recession on the already weakened economy of the region.[26]

In these circumstances, a new federal constitution was eventually agreed upon, under which Flanders, Wallonia and Brussels would all have 'considerable autonomy'. Yet, paradoxically, this has only served to reinforce secessionist demands and to deepen the political divisions between Flanders and Wallonia.

Scottish Nationalism and Crisis Formation in Britain

In 1945 much of the fixed capital in the means of production and circulation in Scotland was well overdue for renewal, but by the early
1960s very little had yet been done to modernise the Scottish
economy. As a consequence, the first effects of international technical
progress resulting in the cheapening of fixed capital were beginning to
appear in Scotland as concentrations of obsolete capacity. A process
of de-industrialisation started and at the same time State fuel policies
began to result in a considerable contraction in capacity and employment in coal-mining and associated activities. Moreover, like the Belgian
economy, the Scottish economy had an outdated structure; many 'new
industries' were 'missing' from it.

It was to combat the resulting weaknesses and stagnation that a
number of business interests drew up a detailed programme of economic modernisation.[27] This called for greatly increased State expenditures to restore the profitability of existing industry, attract new
investment and raise levels of personal and collective consumption. The
essentials of this programme were adopted shortly afterwards by the
then Conservative government.[28] The modernisation of the Scottish
economy was now said to be an essential element of a new regional
policy for the whole British economy, the main aim of which was to
secure 'balanced' regional economic growth.[29] To ensure that this
would occur, a deliberate, rapid expansion of public expenditure in
depressed regions like Scotland was initiated.

In fact, this programme was not too dissimilar from the policies
being advocated at the time by the Labour Party and the Scottish TUC.
In effect, there was broad agreement that major economic reforms
were urgently necessary to modernise the Scottish economy. Thus there
was a definite 'regionalist' response to the increasing problems of the
Scottish economy but it was 'contained' within existing British political
life and institutional arrangements. Demands for action were met by a
rapid expansion of State expenditures.

One of the limitations of the 1963 plan for modernising the Scottish
economy was that it did not deal systematically with places outside
the main industrial and coalfield areas. Policies advanced by the Labour
governments after 1964 sought to remedy this defect through the establishment of a new State agency, the Highlands and Islands Development
Board, and new machinery to permit indicative planning for the whole
Scottish economy.

The new, revised programme for economic growth and modernisation in Scotland put forward by the Labour government in 1966[30] also

assumed that a deliberate, rapid expansion in public expenditure would, after a relatively short time, create conditions where 'self-sustaining' economic growth based on enhanced profitability and competitiveness would start to occur. Once that point had been reached, there would be no further requirement for State expenditures on the scale needed in the 'transition' period during which the structure of the Scottish economy would be thoroughly modernised.

This proposition was seriously upset by events. In fact, it quickly became apparent that the modernisation programmes had all underestimated the severity of the crisis being experienced in most sectors of manufacturing in Scotland. This, combined with the continued and unexpectedly rapid contraction of coal-mining, resulted in unanticipatedly high demands for increased State expenditures within Scotland. At the same time, similar demands suddenly emerged in other regions in Britain and from many hitherto profitable branches of British industry. All this coincided with a succession of balance of payments and sterling crises which were met by a series of cutbacks in public expenditure.

In these circumstances, the regional modernisation programmes first put forward in 1963 and subsequently elaborated by the Labour government, which were intended to transform the depressed regions in Britain, including Scotland, were suddenly abandoned. Unemployment in these regions increased sharply. Since the initial consensus as to what had to be done to modernise the Scottish economy was very broad, the rapid collapse of the modernisation programmes in practice and the accelerated deterioration in much of the Scottish economy were 'obvious' to a wide variety of interests and to a large section of the Scottish electorate, which had been promised considerable improvements in standards of living as part of the modernisation process.

Up to this time, when the main interests representing capital and labour in Scotland had wished to press sectional or indeed consensual policies and demands on central governments, this had been done through the existing British political system which usually accommodated 'regionalist' pressure by increasing public expenditure. With the obvious failure of the British State to meet the requirements of Scottish capital for a restoration of profitability or to meet demands for full employment and increased working-class consumption, another option began to be opened up. This option was for a new alliance of interests to be formed around the Scottish National Party which did not make any significant electoral impact until the collapse of the modernisation policies in 1967, precisely when the 'new nationalism' made its first breakthrough.

The success of the SNP in 1967 shocked the Labour Cabinet and triggered a desperate search for a means of containing the 'nationalist threat'.[31] The government finally decided on a delaying device. A Royal Commission on the constitution was established with the intention of defusing nationalist demands. At first this seemed to have worked since at the 1970 general election, the SNP made much less headway than had been expected. Then, with alarming suddenness, a second and much larger wave of electoral support for the SNP emerged during 1974. This coincided with the publication of the findings of the Royal Commission[32] which were, therefore, immediately taken up by the new, minority, Labour government which also rushed through legislation to establish a Scottish Development Agency.[33]

Subsequently, electoral support for the SNP continued to grow at an even faster rate than previously. Each response by the government to nationalist demands added credibility to the SNP and gave rise to fresh demands. It began to appear that a new form of regionalist bargaining had been established. Sections of the interests representing Scottish capital began to support the SNP and splits began to emerge in the Labour Party in Scotland.[34] A major political realignment in Scotland seemed to be imminent.

It was, therefore, vitally necessary for the Labour government to continue to deliver new benefits and concessions to Scotland under the old-style regionalist politics. This, of course, depended upon the government's ability further to expand or to reallocate expenditure and to carry its supporters from other regions in Britain.

Accordingly, a Development Agency was quickly established and a Bill introduced to establish an elected Assembly in Scotland but neither policy was free from destabilising consequences. In the case of the Development Agency, it was impossible to estimate how much would have to be spent to halt the, by now, rapid decline of the Scottish economy. Moreover, the establishment of the Agency meant that a potentially huge gap would be opened up between Scotland and other depressed regions in England. The whole basis of the regional policy that had lasted since 1945 and which had been claimed as being one of the great achievements of the Labour Party in Britain was, necessarily, being sacrificed by a Labour government. This aroused strong opposition from government supporters with constituencies in depressed areas in England.

The government's proposals for an elected Assembly provoked even greater hostility than the establishment of a separate Development

Agency for Scotland. Again, opposition was particularly fierce from
Labour parties in depressed areas in England. For a time the devolution legislation threatened to paralyse parliamentary business. However,
the Scotland Act was eventually passed and it seemed as if the devolution policy had effectively reduced electoral support for the SNP and at
the same time revived support for the Labour Party in Scotland.[35] One
difficulty remained: an advisory referendum had to be held which must
show clear support for the Act in Scotland before it could be imple-
mented.[36]

When the referendum was held, on 1 March 1979, only 51.5 per cent
of the votes cast supported the proposal for an elected Assembly, while
48.5 per cent opposed it. This result immediately precipitated a
political crisis, since the minority Labour government could not be
confident of avoiding the repeal of the Act because of the strong opposition to its provisions within the Parliamentary Labour Party. At the
same time, it had counted on SNP support to remain in office. Moreover, to avoid delivering devolution would not only precipitate a
general election at a time that the government would not have chosen,
it would also over a longer period threaten to give rise to a new upsurge
of nationalist sentiment in Scotland. Failure to establish an Assembly,
after ten years, would be seen as a disastrous confirmation of the unre-
formable character of the British State and hence could greatly increase
support for a policy of secession which, in turn, would lead to the
break-up of the British State.

As well as adding to the immediate destabilisation of British political
life, the latest round of activity designed to defuse nationalist demands
may also, paradoxically, have altered their character. In the
referendum: 'The central, industrialised regions and the underdeveloped Highlands were for Scottish autonomy. It was small-town
farming Scotland – often depicted as the mainstay of Nationalism –
which got cold feet'.[37] The campaign against the Assembly was
organised and heavily supported by a section of Scottish business
interests, which clearly had no desire to countenance even the establishment of an elected Assembly with only limited powers over the
Scottish economy. Yet the SNP has been a 'bourgeois-nationalist
party'. Thus, the party 'discovered – in the most painful and embar-
rassing fashion – that it [had] no bourgeoisie behind it'.[38] Instead,
support for a limited form of autonomy was strongest in the Scottish
working class.

The SNP was not nearly radical enough to take advantage of this
new situation and, indeed, appears to be incapable of undergoing the

changes which would allow it to catch up with events. Nevertheless, the transformation of the base of support for demands for limited autonomy, combined with continuing industrial and economic decline, may have opened the way towards a radicalisation of Scottish political life which was certainly not the intention in 1974 when the policy of devolution was adopted.

In the general election called after the Labour government failed to carry its devolution policy, support for the SNP collapsed to the levels of 1970 and there was a small swing to Labour in Scotland in marked contrast to the results in the rest of Britain. The new Conservative administration is pledged to repeal the Scotland Act, thereby ignoring the outcome of the March referendum. It is also determined to implement changes in industrial and regional policies, designed to reduce public expenditure, that will almost certainly accelerate the already serious de-industrialisation in Scotland.

As a consequence, pre-conditions are again being created for the emergence of an upsurge of nationalist sentiment but, on this occasion, it is likely to take on new political forms since the credibility and appeal of the SNP have been badly damaged. Clearly, radicalisation of Scottish political life would pose an unprecedented threat to the unity of the British State. Hence devolution policy, even though it had the immediate effect of destroying support for the SNP, may well have only strengthened longer-term pressures for the break-up of Britain.

Lorraine and the Nord: Crisis Formation in France

In contrast to the drawn-out character of the rise of nationalist politics and associated crisis tendencies in Belgium and Scotland, in France a regionalist movement of great strength suddenly emerged during late 1978 and early 1979. By the end of March, this movement had become so generalised that it was beginning to pose a threat to the stability of the French State.[39]

Since 1974 the steel industry in France has been in crisis. In 1977, the French State made its first attempt to secure a reorganisation of the industry. In return for State loans, the major private companies, Usinor, Sacilor and Chiers-Chatillon, promised not to open any further new capacity, undertook to begin a capacity closure programme directed mainly at plant in Lorraine and Nord-Pas-de-Calais and declared 16,000 redundancies to take effect over the next two years. Employment in the industry actually fell by over 16,000 within a year but, even so, nothing seemed to halt the slide of the Sacilor and Usinor companies towards bankruptcy. Hence in September 1978, at the insistence of the French State, a major financial reconstruction of the industry was undertaken. Part of the new agreement was that in return for further massive financial assistance from the State, the companies would draw up and speedily implement a new and more drastic round of redundancies and capacity closures.[40]

Accordingly, a savage closure programme was announced in December 1978 which again severely affected Lorraine and Nord-Pas-de-Calais. On 10 December, Sacilor announced that between April 1979 and the end of 1980, 8,500 jobs would be lost through closure of old iron- and steel-making plant.[41] Shortly afterwards, the Usinor group announced over 12,000 redundancies to be concentrated at Denain, Longwy and Valenciennes (see Table 2.1).[42]

These announcements triggered an immediate reaction in the areas worst threatened by closures and redundancies. Opposition to the companies' decisions was particularly strong in Longwy. This was because the Chiers-Chatillon company, under the terms of the State 'plan' for the

Table 2.1: Proposed Redundancies under the 1978 Plan for the French Steel Industry

Company	Location	Redundancies
Usinor	Denain	5,600
Chiers-Chatillon	Valenciennes	550
	Sedan	100
	Billemont	95
	Longwy	7,200
	Anzin	400
	Blagny	460
Sacilor	Grandrange-Rombas	2,000
	Hagondange	2,200
	Saint Jacques-Hayange	800
	Joeuf-Homécourt	1,050
	Hayange	170
Sollac	Seremange	1,100
	Ebange	1,100
	Florange	1,100
	Fensch	250

Source: *Le Figaro*, 6 February 1979, p. 9.

industry, were required to reduce capacity at Longwy so as to be able to complete a new plant at Neuves-Maison.[43] The unions in the iron and steel and iron-ore mining industries in Lorraine were, therefore, 'provoked' into quickly organising opposition to the closures and a 24-hour general strike was called in the region for 12 January 1979.[44]

The general strike received extremely wide support throughout the region. A large demonstration demanding the cessation of the closure plan was held in Metz together with numerous smaller demonstrations in other towns in the region. Trains moving between Paris and Luxemburg were halted along with all traffic into and out of Hayange and Rombas.[45] At the same time, conventional regionalist politics were also being used to 'persuade' the Barre government and the President of the Republic to drop the closure plans. The Socialist Party, for instance, made three main demands: (1) guarantees of re-employment should be given to all those made redundant; (2) the regions should be re-industrialised by the introduction of new industries; and (3) the tertiary sector should be developed.

The sort of programme implied by these demands had, of course, been used in the past to convert coalfield areas during the 1960s and was already under consideration by the Barre government. The difficulty was that there were insufficient resources available to the French State to allow the problems that had so suddenly emerged in the Nord and Lorraine to be fully met by a 'normal' reconversion policy.[46]

On 16 January the government made an announcement that up to 11,600 jobs would be created in the two regions by 1982. It had been decided, for reasons which are not entirely clear, that most of the limited amount of new industrial investment and employment available should be directed to the Nord.[47] Hardly any new employment was promised for Lorraine (see Table 2.2). Moreover, whereas it was certain that all of the announced redundancies would take place before the end of 1980, the build-up of employment in the new industries was by no means guaranteed. Nor would the government make it certain that workers made redundant from the steel industry would be re-employed in the new industries.

Paradoxically, far from satisfying the demands arising in the Nord, the government's proposals greatly increased opposition to the closure plans. In Lorraine, popular opinion was incensed at what was widely seen to be a derisory gesture by the government. As a consequence, a further general strike was called in the region for 16 February. However, on this occasion, the example of Lorraine was followed by unions in the Nord and a general strike timed to coincide with the Lorraine strike was organised. In addition, the regional general strikes were to be linked to a one-day national strike in the whole French steel industry. Meanwhile, in the Longwy area, direct action and civil

Table 2.2: The French Government's Reconversion Programme, January 1979

Region/Company	New Employment New Plant	in Extension	Town
Nord-Pas-de-Calais (6,800)			
Peugeot-Citroën	2,500		Valenciennes
Française de mécanique	1,400		Douvrin
Société de transmission automatique	200		Ritz
Biderman	600		Cambrai
Biderman		300	Aulnoy-lès-Valenciennes
Corona		157	Valenciennes
Sovati	250		Hordain et Saint Saulve
Erad	100		Aniche
Sofanor		50	Quiévrechain
Bera		40	Haspres et Noyelles
Dangre-Starnord		75	Valenciennes
Rémy		50	Somain
Duvant		50	Saultain
Outinord		55	Saint Amand-les-Eaux
SNCF	1,000		Lille
Lorraine (925)			
General Motors	600		Sarreguemines
STAE	100		Gorcy
Cimiec	50		Ennery
Mus	50		Ennery
Sodelec		75	Fontoy
Moniton	50		Baroncourt
Ardennes (1,350)			
Peugeot-Citroën		350	Charleville
Peugeot-Citroën	1,000		Charleville

Source: *Le Figaro*, 6 February 1979, p. 9.

disobedience began to escalate. Banks and offices as well as factories connected with the steel companies were occupied.

In turn, this drove the government to try to allocate further resources from its already overstretched budget to try to make its reconversion 'offer' more acceptable. To the dismay of the Cabinet, just before the second round of general strikes in Lorraine and the Nord was due to begin, demonstrations against mounting unemployment and redundancies began to break out in yet more regions in France. As a consequence, expenditure had to be switched once more to try to contain this new threat.

As a result, the government was unable to stop the second series of general strikes in the Nord and Lorraine which were accompanied by

very large demonstrations and led to a massive upsurge in direct action
to block roads and railways, to disrupt trade and to close the frontier
between France and Belgium.[48] There was also unanimous support for
the national strike in the steel industry.

By now the government was starting to lose control of the situation
in the Nord and Lorraine.[49] Direct action tactics began to be widely
adopted throughout the two regions. Moreover, the movements in the
Nord and Lorraine began to become aware of their international
significance: 'Les futurs chômeurs europeéens savant à présent qu'ils
peuvent, s'ils le veulent, paralyser toute une région.'[50]

After the second general strike in Lorraine, the government declared
that it would stand firm on the implementation of its plan for the steel
industry, otherwise it would be impossible to maintain international
competitiveness and this would affect growth throughout the French
economy. At the same time, violent incidents began to increase in parts
of Lorraine. The most serious occurred on the evening of 23 February
and the early morning of 24 February when police halted the occupation of a local television station which had been taken over by
'militants'. Subsequently, the local police commissariat was besieged
by over 2,000 demonstrators. Meanwhile, the opposition to the government's plan for the steel industry began to become yet more generalised and transformed into widespread antagonism to the government's
whole economic policy[51] and especially to the continued rise in
unemployment.

Early in March, the most serious upsurge of civil disorder that had
yet occurred took place in Denain in the Nord.[52] Steelworkers in
Denain, imitating the tactics devised in Longwy, blocked a number of
roads around the town. The aim was to bring attention to the planned
redundancies at the Denain plant which were then the subject of a new
round of negotiations in Paris. However, unlike previous occasions and
probably as a result of the previous events in Longwy and Sedan, on
Tuesday 6 March the CRS riot police were ordered into Denain. Pickets
blocking a road were attacked and badly beaten.

The next day, a large demonstration to protest against the involvement of the CRS took place outside the police commissariat. According
to eyewitnesses, the CRS again attacked the demonstrators but on this
occasion were themselves attacked in turn. Throughout the rest of the
day and most of the night, a pitched battle was fought in the streets.
The following day, the CRS were withdrawn and although sporadic
violence continued, most of the workers decided to occupy the steel-
works rather than prolong the street fighting.

These events now presented a clear threat to the continuation of the government's steel plan and constituted the most serious breakdown in public order in France since May 1968. Yet the government was not in a position to abandon its plan for the steel industry, since to do so might threaten accumulation in the whole French economy. Nor was the government in a position to increase the size of the reconversion programme on offer. This was because extra spending would have destroyed the general deflationary policy of the Barre government, a policy which was considered to be necessary to restore the balance of payments equilibrium. This left the State with the option of repression to coerce opposition in the two regions into acceptance of the steel plan. However, the intervention of the CRS in Denain only provoked a further escalation in the crisis.

Thus an initially 'simple' regional problem brought about by the necessary restructuring of a key sector in the French economy had, within three months, been transformed into a condition of unprecedented social crisis in the Nord and Lorraine. In addition, the crises in these two regions had begun to destabilise French political life and to pose a direct challenge to the authority of the State.

Concluding Remarks

According to the interpretation put forward in this chapter, regional problems are a permanent and necessary consequence of or pre-condition for capital accumulation. Yet regional problems also threaten to disrupt accumulation. In late capitalism, State intervention in regional problems seeks to resolve this contradiction. However, in most European countries the deepening entanglement of the State in regional problems has, in fact, coincided with their deterioration and has only served to amplify and generalise regional crisis tendencies.

The failures of State intervention in regional problems have given rise to opportunities for the establishment and growth of new nationalist and regionalist movements which have begun to precipitate acute disruption of 'normal' political activity in several European countries. Such disruption has still further eroded the effectiveness of State interventions in regional problems.

Since the onset of the international recession in 1974, regional crisis tendencies have begun to be expressed in a growing number of regions in Europe. Indeed, some regional crises have served to trigger the formation of much wider crises and this specific path of crisis formation seems likely to become even more important in the future. The new nationalist and regionalist movements associated with regional crises may not be able to acquire sufficient support to gain power, but these movements are likely to prove increasingly capable of further curbing the effectiveness of State interventions in accumulation. If so, this is certain to threaten the coherence of late capitalism in at least some of the most advanced countries in Europe.

Notes

1. The exchange value of a commodity may be defined as the amount of socially necessary labour time required to produce it.

2. E. Mandel, *Late Capitalism* (New Left Books, London, 1975), p. 438.

3. This conclusion was in some dispute up to the onset of the general international recession in 1974 which has provided overwhelming evidence as to the instability of capital accumulation on a world scale. See E. Mandel, *The Second Slump* (New Left Books, London, 1978) and Giovanni Arrighi's paper, 'Towards a Theory of Capitalist Crisis', *New Left Review*, no. 111 (1978), pp. 3-24.

4. The mechanisms of an industrial cycle and of the formation of an overproduction crisis are described by Mandel in his *Late Capitalism*, p. 439 as follows:

> An economic upswing is possible only with a rising rate of profit, which in turn creates the conditions for a fresh extension of the market and an accentuation of the upswing. At a certain point in this development, however, the increased organic composition of capital and the limit to the number of commodities that can be sold to 'final consumers' must lower the rate of profit and also induce a contraction of the market. These contractions then spill over into a crisis of overproduction.

Investment is curtailed due to the fall in the rate of profit 'turning the downswing into a depression'. The devalorisation of capital and increasing unemployment and rationalisation create conditions whereby the rate of profit can begin to rise again. 'The decline in output and depletion of stock permit a new expansion of the market, which combines with the recovery of the rate of profit to restimulate investments and hence to launch an upswing in production.'

In an economy comprising two departments of production, in the upswing phase, the rate of profit grows more rapidly in Department I than in Department II. In a downswing, over-capacity becomes most acute in Department I. Recovery is led by Department II where the rate of profit had fallen less than in Department I. This account suggests that accumulation crises are to some extent self-correcting, in the sense that the recession following a boom creates preconditions for a subsequent recovery. There is, however, no guarantee that a recovery will necessarily carry output, employment, investment and capacity to higher levels than hitherto achieved. Long-period real growth will only occur in circumstances where there is an 'undertone of expansion'. Nor is there any certainty as to the low point that will actually be reached in a recession. Hence it is quite possible that accumulation crises will be 'explosive' in their character. This is why State intervention to damp down and to anticipate and avoid accumulation crises has become a central feature of late capitalism.

5. Two other important characteristics of accumulation in late capitalism are: (i) the reduction in the turnover time of fixed capital and (ii) the heightened con-

centration and centralisation of capital.

The reduction in the turnover time of fixed capital has come to be of considerable importance in maintaining and increasing the rate of profit and hence in sustaining and accelerating accumulation. Concentration and centralisation tendencies in late capitalism are now increasingly expressed internationally. Thus multinational companies have become the main 'unit of capital' in late capitalism and, as a corollary, direct investment is now the main form of foreign investment.

6. Mandel in his *Marxist Economic Theory* (2 vols., Merlin Press, London, 1968), vol. 1, p. 373, argues that 'unevenness of development as between different parts of a single country' is an essential pre-condition for capital accumulation and, moreover, has usually been greatly underestimated in Marxist writing. Mandel points out that 'by creating depressed areas within the capitalist nations, the capitalist mode of production itself creates its own "complementary" markets as well as permanent reserves of labour-power.'

7. The response of Italian capital to this crisis was a 'nature-like', unplanned 'diffuse industrialisation' of the Central and North-Eastern regions in Italy.

8. The planned industrialisation of the Mezzogiorno is analysed in great detail by Augusto Graziani in his major study, *Investimenti Autonomi e Investimenti Indotti nell' Economia del Mezzogiorno* (University of Naples, Naples, 1977).

9. The 'opening up' of depressed rural areas through State intervention could be interpreted as a vital step in expanding the market for capitalist production and hence in laying the basis for rapid accumulation in the manufacturing sector. The destruction of the existing economy in such areas, assisted by State intervention, may well have been the only true purpose of such intervention in many cases. See, for example, Graziani's comments on this issue in *Investimenti Autonomi*.

10. The consequences for countries drawn into this system were to perpetuate their economic backwardness and eventually to destabilise their economies, issues discussed in J. Berger and J. Mohr, *A Seventh Man* (Penguin, Harmondsworth, 1975).

11. This is discussed by Läpple and Hoogstraten in Chapter 6 of this book and also Hans Geraets and Frits Wegenwijs in their paper, 'Het Industrialisatieproces in Midden-Zeeland', *Zone*, no. 8 (1978), pp. 15-57.

12. There is considerable empirical evidence to support this thesis. See, for example, Carney and Hudson, *State Regional Policies and Uneven Development: the Case of the North East* (Centre for Environmental Studies, London, 1979).

13. See, for example, Graziani's *Investimenti Autonomi* and also C. Chinello, *Storia Di Uno Sviluppo Capitalistico: Porto Marghera E Venezia, 1951-1973* (Editori Riuniti, Rome, 1975).

14. This is discussed in detail in a book by the author, *De-Industrialisation in Britain after 1965: the Regional Impact* (in preparation).

15. Conventionally, regional problems are also said to occur in areas where there has been rapid economic growth involving expansion in population, output, employment, capacity and consumption. Such regions are said to suffer from the problems of the 'negative externalities' of growth which are expressed in specifically regional inflation due to labour and infrastructure shortages. Clearly such problems may again be interpreted as arising from accumulation imperatives.

Capital accumulation requires the expansion of capacity and the assembly of extra labour forces over relatively short periods of time. Advances in accumulation require considerable volumes of labour migration to areas of rapid growth along with expansion of raw materials circulation and consumption. However, there is no guarantee that arrangements to meet these requirements will be sufficiently well co-ordinated to eliminate the possibility of capacity bottlenecks, labour shortages or the underprovision of infrastructure. Hence there is always a danger that accumulation will break down in the regions where growth is most rapid due to the effects of the local inflation generated by shortages of all kinds.

16. Between 1955 and 1963, Italian economic development was particularly rapid. It was concentrated in one region, the North-West, and based on the expansion of exports from both 'traditional' and 'modern' sectors. To remain competitive, given the available technology in these sectors, it was necessary for wages to grow less quickly than productivity. This was made possible by a huge labour migration to the North-West from the peripheral regions in Italy. Nevertheless, after a period of very rapid expansion, infrastructure shortages in the North-West began to appear along with a rapid rise in the cost of living. This led to a severe crisis in the region. Wage demands put forward first by the unsocialised Southern migrants and then taken up by the 'labour aristocracy' in the region threatened to completely disrupt accumulation. This was avoided partly through the decentralisation of production to the North-Eastern and Central regions, where existing social conditions permitted a rapid 'diffuse industrialisation' based on small and medium-sized enterprises.

This industrialisation allowed wage costs to be controlled and hence permitted continued expansion in exports from the 'traditional sector'. This was because social conditions in the North-Eastern and Central regions allowed wages to be reduced and greatly increased labour flexibility. At the same time, the form of industrialisation that occurred, based on small and medium-sized enterprises, did not disrupt the existing social conditions, but rather guaranteed their preservation.

17. E. Mandel, 'The Dialectic of Class and Region in Belgium, *New Left Review*, no. 20 (1963), pp. 5-31. The account of the 1960-1 crisis in Belgium given here draws heavily on Mandel's paper.

18. Between 1955 and 1960, GDP in Belgium only grew at a rate of 2.3 per cent per annum. This was a much lower growth rate than in West Germany (6.4 per cent), France (4.8 per cent), or the Netherlands (4.5 per cent); see D.T. Jones, 'Output, Employment and Labour Productivity in Europe Since 1955', *National Institute Economic Review*, no. 77 (August 1976), p. 80.

19. Mandel, 'The Dialectic of Class and Region in Belgium', p. 19.

20. Ibid.

21. This industry produced locomotives, coaches and trams.

22. Mandel, 'The Dialectic of Class and Region in Belgium', p. 26.

23. This marked a major shift in working-class politics and political life in Wallonia:

For over fifty years the Walloon workers had cared about only one issue, the social question. Through the different organisations of the Socialist movement they fought to establish a socialist society. There was no cultural problem for them, for they were not victimised by any cultural or linguistic discrimination. Their language (French) was, on the contrary, the dominant language in the country (Mandel, 'The Dialectic of Class and Region in Belgium', p. 17).

24. The regional economy in Flanders grew at twice the rate of the economy in Wallonia in the sixties.

25. The aim was to establish largely self-governing regions leaving only limited powers to the central government.

26. It was reported early in March 1979 that

Wallonia is getting close to the politics of despair. Walloons find it hard to accept the reality that the formerly underprivileged Flemish are now bankers to Belgium and are both the more numerous and economically prosperous group in the country. The somewhat incoherent thought behind secession seems to be that the ensuing chaos would shock the Flemings into compromise (*Financial Times*, 2 March 1979).

27. Scottish Council (Development and Industry), *Inquiry into the Scottish Economy* (James Paton, Dundee, 1961).

28. Scottish Development Department, *Central Scotland: a Programme for Development and Growth*, Cmnd. 2188 (HMSO, Edinburgh, 1963).

29. *H.C. Deb, (Hansard)*, vol. 685 (1963), cols. 985-1003.

30. Scottish Office, *The Scottish Economy 1965 to 1970: a Plan for Expansion*, Cmnd. 2864 (HMSO, Edinburgh, 1966).

31. Some allusions to this are found in Richard Crossman's *The Diaries of a Cabinet Minister* (3 vols., Hamish Hamilton and Jonathan Cape, London, 1975, 1976, 1977), vol. 2, pp. 550-1 and p. 610. At this time a number of hitherto safe Labour-held seats in South Wales as well as in Scotland seemed to be threatened by a combination of the sudden upsurge in nationalist sentiment and support and the unprecedented unpopularity of the Labour government. See also K. Buchanan, 'The Revolt Against Satellization in Scotland and Wales', *Monthly Review*, vol. 18 (1967), pp. 36-48.

32. Royal Commission on the Constitution, 1969-1973, *Report*, Cmnd. 5460 (HMSO, London, 1973), Vol. II.

33. For the first time, the Secretary of State, through the SDA, would become permanently involved in and obviously responsible for the 'performance' of the Scottish economy: 'The Bill is one of historic significance to Scotland. It is the first to confer on a Secretary of State for Scotland substantial powers in relation to Scottish industry' (*H.C. Deb. (Hansard)*, vol. 894 (1975), col. 464.

34. The discovery of North Sea oil greatly added to the credibility of the SNP's claims concerning the viability of an independent Scottish State. It also altered the class interests represented by the SNP. The party began to attract the support of Edinburgh-based financial and commercial interests involved in investment trusts and merchant banks expecting to make great gains from economic activity and speculation associated with the development of the North Sea reserves. Thus the party came to represent the interests of the most self-confident section of the Scottish bourgeoisie which could readily envisage the benefits of controlling the flows of finance and revenues connected with the North Sea through the establishment of a separate Scottish State. At the same time, these financial and commercial interests were not 'desperate', hence their support for the SNP was not subsequently whole-hearted or consistent.

35. Electoral support for the SNP was weak in all three Parliamentary by-elections held in Scotland in 1978.

36. An amendment to the Act meant that the government would have to make an Order repealing it if fewer than 40 per cent of the Scottish electorate voted 'Yes' in the referendum.

37. T. Nairn, 'What Really Happened in Scotland', *New Statesman*, 9 March 1979, p. 313.

38. Ibid.

39. These events which at the time of writing (late March 1979), threatened to become 'an industrial 1968' were all the more remarkable since in 1978 the left were apparently soundly defeated in the general election and the Barre government subsequently appeared to be very secure.

40. The aim was to convert most of the steel companies' massive debt (40 billion francs) into State-owned share capital. Arrangements were also made to

guarantee interest payments on steel industry bonds. The government emphasised that State control over the industry was only intended to be 'temporary'.

41. Capacity at Hagondange, Hayange and Homécourt was to be closed or partially closed.

42. Smaller companies, such as Paris-Outreau and Creusot-Loire, also announced redundancies.

43. This seems to have been on the grounds that the Longwy work-force were unlikely to challenge the closure decision.

44. The campaign slogan was: 'Défendons La Lorraine.'

45. *Le Monde*, 13 January 1979, p. 1 and p. 26.

46. *Le Figaro*, 9 January 1979, p. 5.

47. It is possible that the government was hoping to secure the new Ford car assembly plant for Lorraine. To have moved other employment into Lorraine might have prejudiced this project. See *Le Figaro*, 17 January 1979, p. 9.

48. In Sedan, demonstrators even attacked the local police commissariat.

49. Molotov cocktails were used by demonstrators as the violence escalated and, after dark, shots were fired at the CRS.

50. A young worker at a picket blocking the motorway to Wallonia told *Le Monde*: 'Nous avons découvert une nouvelle forme de guérilla urbaine.'

51. *Le Monde*, 18-19 February 1979, p. 19.

52. The following account is based on reports appearing in *Le Figaro, Le Monde* and other European newspapers.

3 THE STRUCTURATION OF SPACE, THE PROBLEM OF LAND, AND SPATIAL POLICY

Alain Lipietz

Background to the Problem

The 'space' under discussion is the object of study of human geography, economic geography and theories of spatial economics alike and is also the object upon which spatial policy and regional action are practised. This 'space' is the material form of existence of the socio-economic relations which structure social formations, and, in particular, French society.

Any social formation is a complex structure of social relationships, linked at the level of the economic, legal-political and ideological instances. It appears as an articulation of combinations — types of relationships linked at the level of these three instances and determined by the relationships of production, combinations called *modes of production* (capitalism, petty commodity production, domestic production, feudalism . . .). But this articulation is not a linear combination: on the one hand, the form of existence of each of the modes is considerably modified by the place allotted to it by the reproduction of the dominant mode in the social formation (capitalism); on the other hand, the dominant mode of production itself includes among its concrete conditions of existence, in the formation under consideration, the presence of other modes of production (which provide it with reserves of labour, market outlets, etc.). If each of the modes of production possesses *a priori* its own *dynamic* of development, its own logic, generally in contradiction to that of other modes, whose presence is revealed by analysis, it appears that after synthesis, in the concrete articulation of the modes, the dominance of the capitalist mode of production imposes its *unity* on the whole, its mode of functioning which appears '*ex post*' coherent. Analysis will thus reveal, for example, the antagonism of an 'industrial logic' corresponding to the advanced forms of capitalism, opposed to a 'property logic' characteristic of archaic modes, but concrete examination will reveal on the ground the functioning of a unique and coherent system possessing distinctive characteristics. To explain these is precisely the aim of analysis. In fact the actual conditions of the articulation must be understood as a *process* in which the dominant mode dominates, breaks down and integrates the dominated mode in successive phases in which the working rules of the social totality are modified.

From this conception of social structure a conception of spatial structure also emerges. We believe in fact that concrete socio-economic space can itself be analysed in terms of the articulation of 'spatialities'[1] appropriate to clearly defined relationships in the different instances of different modes of production present in the social formation. What is the nature of this 'spatiality'? It is a form of correspondence between 'presence/absence' (in geographical space) and 'participation/exclusion' in the structure considered. The forms of 'presence/absence' are themselves specified by the structure in question. One can thus speak, for example, of the *economic* space of the capitalist mode of production, relative to the state of the spatial division of labour and to that of transport and telecommunications; or of *legal* space which is superimposed upon it and which takes the form of a cadastral register, fixing for private individuals the limits of the right of use and abuse. We shall see that legal space of this sort, an inheritance of the past social formation, stands in the way of the redeployment of capitalism.

It should be understood that concrete socio-economic space appears both as the articulation of analysed spaces, as a product, a *reflection* of the articulation of social relationships, and at the same time, as far as already existing concrete space is concerned, as an objective constraint imposed upon the redeployment of those social relationships. We shall say that society recreates its space on the basis of a concrete space, always already provided, established in the past. This is how we will tackle the question of territorial development.

Our approach will reflect this problematic. We will first examine the constitution of concrete regional spaces as the product of the articulation of modes of production and then, on the basis of the national space so constituted, we will examine the rules of operation of the system and the problems posed for the development of advanced forms of capitalism, which will enable us to distinguish the objectives of the State.

From the Articulation of Modes of Production to Regional Uneven Development

The Dominant Mode

The capitalist mode of production is characterised by the separation of producers from their means of production and by the private autonomous character of the development of the different parts of social

capital. The law of value, which is imposed by means of market
exchange between these parts, assures the self-regulation of the development of the different branches of production.

Spatially, the redeployment of capitalism will be characterised by
the location of the unit of production (fixed capital) as a function of a
calculation of private profitability, bearing in mind the capacity for
appropriation of the objects of labour and of labour power in the form
of commodities, and for disposal of the products in a market. It is
necessary to enquire whether there is any law of spatial self-regulation
equivalent to the law of value for the distribution of capital and social
labour among the branches and we shall see that this is only very
partially the case. But, from the very fact that the management of
capitalist development presents a private character for each autonomous part of capital, we shall only be able to examine this problem
after analysing the concrete spatial framework (which constitutes what
Perroux would call 'plan contents' of the agents dominating the processes of capitalist development).[2] However, it should be remembered
that, considered globally, the capitalist mode of production assigns a
double function to other modes of production in its development:

a reservoir of labour freed by their disintegration;
an outlet for its products and a field of investment for its development.

In its historical development the capitalist mode of production has
gone through several successive stages in different branches, which can
be superimposed on each other geographically or exclude each other —
in particular through the mode of occupation of the land, the structure
acquired by the labour market, etc. The periodisation of the succession
of stages is relative to the labour process (stages of manufacture, large-
scale industry, automation) and to the process of valorisation of capital
(competitive and monopolistic stages). These different stages also have
their own spatiality. In particular, advanced forms of capitalism are
characterised by a geographical separation of the labour process and the
process of valorisation of capital. The increasing independence of
finance capital and of research and development activities in fact allows
the monopolistic sectors to regulate the spatial division of labour
between centres of innovation and research, manufacturing centres and
assembly centres, as a function of a distribution of supply centres and of
a transport system, of labour resources and of markets which can,
moreover, be either pre-existing or rearranged. It is no longer, therefore,

as in neo-classical economics, a question of supporting or rejecting hypotheses about 'mobility of factors' but of proceeding with an analysis of regional structures which specifies the conditions of deployment of modern capitalist activity.

The Dominated Modes and their Process of Articulation with the Capitalist Mode of Production (CMP)

Here we will treat the remains of the feudal mode of production, such as great landed estates cultivated by tenant farmers, as negligible. Let us merely point out that this type of property offers fewest problems to capitalist expansion, in that its type of transfer of surplus labour can easily take on monetary forms corresponding to the dominant economic rationality and the elimination of superfluous agricultural population is very rapid in such cases.

Nor will we become preoccupied with an economic form which is not a true mode of production since it would be incapable of autonomous existence: domestic production. Let us note, however, that this 'domestic quasi-mode of production', functioning as an auxiliary to the capitalist mode of production or to petty commodity production, represents one of the principal reserves for capitalism, both as a reserve army of wage labour and as a potential outlet for new capitalist products (ready-made clothing, convenience foods, electrical household goods, etc.). The first aspect has undoubted importance in territorial development, especially in view of the 'liberation' of family labour from small agricultural production for work in decentralised factories.

We are going to concentrate (from the point of view of its regional influence) on agricultural petty commodity production. In this mode, the worker himself is proprietor and possessor of his means of production (he chooses how they are to be allocated and sets them to work himself); the aim (the logic) of production is the simple reproduction of the unit of operation. One of the means of production is the land. The form of spatial existence of this mode is the overlaying of an economic space and a legal space, both divided into small lots, and consisting of the juxtaposition of family-operated units organised round market towns.

The articulation of this mode with the CMP passes through a succession of phases. First, the (non-economic) necessity for each generation to repurchase the land forces small-scale production to enter a commercial, monetary relationship with the rest of the economy. This begins the first phase of the articulation, through the intermediary of the market: agriculture provides the CMP with provisions sold at a price which allows the simple reproduction of the agricultural operation, that is 'at cost price'. On the other hand, small-scale agricultural production buys industrial products from capitalism at a price of production which includes capitalist profit. So, an 'unequal exchange' operates, which on the one hand shows a transfer of value towards industry and on the other involves the stagnation of small agricultural production, expressing itself as a brake on industrialisation and in the relative impoverishment of the peasantry.

In general, petty commodity production is none the less a 'tenacious' mode which does not disintegrate easily, since peasants hang on to land which they continue to own. The competition of other modes of agricultural production can induce petty commodity production to increase its degree of mechanisation, and therefore the average area of individual holdings, which causes rural depopulation, but this phenomenon is much more gradual than in areas of large-scale farming. In addition, the phenomenon can be completely prevented by protectionist measures, as was the case under the Third Republic.

However, in a second phase, capitalism penetrates agriculture by means of loans for mechanisation and contracts linking it with the agricultural processing industries. The small producer remains formally independent but in fact it is Crédit Agricole and the agricultural processing industry which dictate the direction of his work. The peasant's turnover increases sharply, but once he has accounted for repayments, loan interest and expenses, he is left with an income which allows him to survive only if combined with subsistence farming. The small operator becomes economically an employee of the processing industry, indeed an underpaid employee considering the conditions of reproduction of his labour power: hence there exists an unequal exchange in a restricted sense between industry and agriculture. This second phase of the articulation is revealed by a speeding up of rural depopulation; at this stage land ownership becomes as great a fetter to the peasant as to capitalism.

We think that this outline[3] has great general applicability. We will call the outline of the first phase an *external articulation*, in which the dominated mode is articulated with capitalism by the intermediary of the circulation of commodities with a transfer of value from one to the other by virtue of the absolute non-payment for the surplus labour incorporated in the products of the first. The stagnation of incomes and re-investment resulting from this in the dominated mode forms the basis of the relationship which develops in the second phase, called the integration phase, in which money capital invests in the branch (or region) dominated by the archaic mode and, without necessarily immediately modifying the legal form, acquires direct control of the allocation of labour and appropriates surplus labour at a relatively higher rate than that of the classic branches of its area of domination.

The Articulation of Regional Spaces

Regional spaces are not principally delimited by legal-political space (in particular by administrative divisions). They must be constructed on the basis of the concrete analysis of modes of production and their articulation. A region is a concrete articulation of spatialities appropriate to different social relationships. Just as there are several levels in the object of an analysis, so there are several levels in regional division. But it is not a question of taking into account empirically a greater or smaller spatial scale. The required scale is determined by socio-economic spatial forms.

Since an economic region is characterised by the dominance of an economic form, we will transpose the above analyses of the articulation of modes on to inter-regional relationships. Thus we can say that *a region is dominated* when it is specialised in branches organised by dominated modes or by archaic stages of the dominant mode. We can say that a region is externally dominated when small independent producers or small and medium-sized local capitalists carry on an unequal exchange with the dominant region by means of the price of commodities. This unequal exchange is a block to autonomous regional capitalist development and tends to lower the social cost of reproduction of labour power. The way is thus prepared for the stage of *integration-domination* when external capital takes control of local production while profiting from the low incomes inherited from the earlier period.

Now, regarding the transfer of the ability to labour from one mode to another, two courses are open to the 'reserve army of labour' made available by the dissolution of the dominated modes: emigration or integration into the wage-labour force in the same place. In the first case, the cost of reproduction of labour power becomes the same as that of the dominant regions (purely capitalist life-style); in the second case for a certain length of time it can remain very much lower, due to the fact that poverty is customary and especially because of the partially extra-capitalist nature of this reproduction (subsistence farming).

From Inter-regional Centre-Periphery Relationships to Industrial Spatial Policy

We have just examined how the process of articulation of the capitalist mode of production and pre- or palaeo-capitalist modes brings about an uneven development of regions, when the regions, for historical reasons, have experienced an uneven domination by the CMP. The result is the stabilisation and the enlarged reproduction of a 'centre-periphery' spatial structure, the capitalist mode of production tending to gain the ascendancy at the centre (embracing all aspects of socio-economic processes), without managing to develop on a local basis in the peripheral regions, on account of the unequal exchange which prevents capitalist accumulation at the periphery. We shall examine how capitalism functions at the centre and in the peripheral regions.

Self-centred Accumulation and Extraverted Accumulation

The law of capitalist development in the 'central' regions is *self-centred accumulation,*[4] that is the development of investment and consumption constantly creates outlets on a local basis for Departments I (producer goods) and II (consumer goods) of production. This is the Marxist scheme of expanded reproduction; it is also the Keynesian equilibrium. The permanent revolution in technological processes and the changing relations of values resulting from it imply that, to maintain equilibrium in the distribution of labour and of social capital, certain relations must be respected, for example that the increasing purchasing power of producers keeps pace with their productivity. But more generally, it is the whole system of branches which must keep to the dynamic inter-relationships which are evident in inter-sectoral input-output matrices.

The dominated regions are characterised, on the other hand, by the model of *extraverted accumulation*: on a local base of ever more restricted simple reproduction (subsistence farming, craft production and small Department II local enterprises), their principal economic activity is the *export sector* (for French regions, essentially agriculture). This sector offers low returns to producers and better ones to the dominant local classes or the local representatives of the dominant central classes. The consumer goods corresponding to the standard of living implied by the incomes of these classes are not generally available locally and must be imported. At the scale of a national structure like France, a single market exists for these products and a regional policy of import substitution is hardly conceivable.

This model presents, therefore, a great *disarticulation* of the local productive system, evident in the regional inter-sectoral input-output matrix. If, furthermore, one is in a phase of integration-domination, that is to say, if the capital invested in the region which extracts the surplus value produced is foreign, then there is no longer even any correspondence between regional product and regional income. Hence it can be seen that the classical mechanisms of self-centred accumulation, grasped by regional theories of Keynesian inspiration in terms of multiplier effects (export base) or accelerator effects (Aftalion effect), are no longer at all pertinent since these effects operate not at the level of the peripheral region but at that of the system as a whole. These regional theories invoke the inequality of marginal propensities for saving or importing: but this is precisely what must be explained.

Establishment of the Branch Circuit

The development of multi-regional (indeed multinational) monopoly capital in the integration-domination phase will proceed, with State aid, on the basis of this spatial polarisation.

We should note initially that the multi-regional character of this development presupposes the autonomy of finance capital and of research activities (which allow the 'delocalisation' of new establishments). Capital which remains in family hands without developing its own research facilities tends to stay isolated in its region of origin.

The utilisation of polarised space by modern capitalist firms tends to set up what we will call a *branch circuit*, by obvious reference to Vernon's[5] 'product cycle'. Vernon takes as his starting-point the demand for a product and observes the temporal variation in policies for location of production with the displacement of the centre of gravity of that demand. We start from the production, not of a single product, but of a group of linked products constituting the branch. The polarisation of space and the increasing autonomy of finance capital and research, together with the development of the transport system, today make it possible to establish an inter-regional division of labour within a single branch, while the network of the different production processes can take the most diverse forms (market transaction, circulation within the firm, patents, subcontracting, etc.). The branch circuit depends on three types of economic region:

(1) those with a highly technological environment, with close links between business centres, innovation centres and centres of research and technological and scientific teaching. 'Externalities' (in relation to the branches) are intense. The value of labour power is important here; so too is the skilled part of the labour force.

(2) those with a high proportion of skilled personnel (technicians, professional workers), which presupposes an industrial tradition corresponding at least to the stage of large-scale industry, and an average value of labour power.

(3) those with reserves of labour which can be regarded as unskilled and as having a very low value of reproduction, since they are produced by the disintegration of other modes or by the decline of obsolete industries corresponding to an earlier stage of the division of labour.

The control centre of the overall system is, in general, region 1, the region of self-centred accumulation, the real centre of the process of valorisation of finance capital and the technological centre of the labour process: this must be a national or international metropolis (Paris region). However, above a certain level of centralisation there is a danger that efficiency will be reduced. It can then be advantageous to reserve the technological direction of the circuit, together with relative financial autonomy, for super-regional metropoles: this is doubtless the future promised for the Lyons metropolis.[6]

The regions of type 3 are the most typically peripheral: they include, for example, regions undergoing the accelerated dissolution of small agricultural production. This industrialisation allowed by the setting up of the branch circuit in no way breaks the rules of extraverted accumulation: on the contrary it conforms to them. 'Self-sufficient' establishments are required, which need few links with others nearby. Not that these are isolated; rather they have their place in the national or world space of the branch. But their connection to the regional space only results from a demand for unskilled labour (in the case of Western France) or from ecological or land ownership situations considered free of constraint (petrochemicals and the Mediterranean iron and steel industry). These establishments seek to avoid local external effects and indeed do not bring about any: they remain 'cathedrals in the desert'.

The regions of type 2 are intermediate. They often involve former centres corresponding to an old inter-regional division of labour, which lacking a diversified and interwoven structure around them, and for reasons to do with the rigidity of ownership of capital, or with the displacement of the profits arising from unequal exchange, could not or would not change: among them the textile and mining areas of the old Europe.

Figure 3.1: French Regions

France: Elements of the Future:

France comprises:

a national or European centre of type 1: the Paris region;
different industrial centres corresponding to the stage of large-scale
industry and to external articulation with pre-capitalist modes: the
metropolitan centres of Lyons and Lille, the old industrial areas
(Nord, Est, Saint-Etienne). These ex-centres may become: either sub-
centres, managing the labour process and the process of super-
regional valorisation of finance capital allocated from Paris or any
other world centre; or industrial regions of type 2, that is regions of
skilled manufacturing;
a mainly agricultural periphery scattered with small towns, small
industries and large importing/exporting ports (Marseilles,
Bordeaux).

What is the future of the agricultural periphery? It depends on the type of articulation which has been attained.

In highly developed regions, the rural exodus follows the classical model of the feudal/capitalist articulation seen in England. It is in this kind of region (in the Paris Basin for example) that the loss of workers from the land has been greatest and continues most rapidly. But such regions can be regarded as having practically exhausted their reserve armies.

In the central and highland regions, the population has greatly decreased through the external articulation, 'petty commodity production/capitalism'. The last survivors of an ageing peasantry are unable to prevent the take-over of land ownership by North European capital in pursuit of its own ends (tourism, etc). Young people leave both countryside and town for centres of types 1 and 2, for these regions have no reserve army of sufficient density to serve as assembly areas in the branch circuit.

In regions like the Bocage of the West, petty commodity production is integrated by capitalism and every year frees large contingents of cultivators and, especially, family labour. The big question is knowing where capital is going to employ this reserve army.

In the period of the external articulation, which corresponded to the stage of large-scale industry, at the competitive stage, 'spontaneous' emigration was the rule (towards the old centres, via the medium-sized local towns). Today integration-domination allows an alternative policy: establishments for unskilled workers in the heart of the branch circuit, located directly in the pool of labour.

It is important not to exaggerate this possibility of local industrialisation either quantitatively or, particularly, qualitatively. Since it depends on the relative cheapness of an unqualified labour force, it can neither be expected to increase incomes greatly, nor to have any training effect. However, it is conceivable that a complete branch circuit might be set up in a super-region focused on a former centre which has remained dynamic (like electronics in the West, centred on Nantes).

The advantage of this new policy is that it leaves both the social and private cost of reproduction of labour power at a low level: it is unnecessary to build new dwellings in congested urban areas, unnecessary to pay in wages what the peasant-worker produces himself, etc.

Let us emphasise, however, that it is neither necessary nor sufficient for a reserve army to be available in a region for monopoly capital to invest the corresponding fixed capital. The former centre of

Lorraine could only be converted with difficulty into a type 2 region, due as much to the traditions of local hegemony of large Lorraine family businesses as to the competition of German wages. Conversely, since the region of Fos contained no pool of labour, immigrants from the Maghreb and Lorraine have provided, and will continue to provide, the labour needed by an industrial/port area, the location of which depends on other considerations (world capacity of iron and steel production, etc.).

Creation and Private Appropriation of Socio-economic Space

We have been examining the constitution of regional spaces through the structure of social relationships and the use made of them by capital as far as the movement of accumulation, split up into branches by the division of labour, is concerned. Now we must examine the problem at the level of the capitalist firm run by a private agent who perceives socio-economic space as given, along with the inter-regional division of labour, the pre-existing materialised fixed capital, the location of markets, the state of the transport and telecommunications system and the structure of legal space (ownership of land).

Absence of a 'Law of Value in Space'

As outlined above, there is always a solution to the problem of the marginal firm seeking an optimal location. Hence the idea of constituting a 'microeconomics in space', which would integrate, in addition to costs and quantities, distances, areas and incomes. However, this attempt soon runs into serious difficulties: there is no Walrasian spatial equilibrium, bearing in mind the importance of externalities.[7]

It should be emphasised from the outset that as soon as space intervenes, 'externalities' (of 'location', within the branch, or of 'urbanisation', external to the branch) become the general rule, since the costs of transport can always be counted as such. This is where the contradiction between the social character of production and the private (autonomous) character of appropriation and economic ownership is expressed at its sharpest in its *material* form. In space, the 'general equivalent' constituted by money in the allocation and reallocation of social labour does not exist. As soon as fixed capital is installed (on private initiative) the field of distances and socio-economic space is irrevocably transformed: by materialising, private capital becomes collective fixed capital. One cannot therefore think of reaching an optimum equilibrium 'through the market'. Economic space, together with the social forces and conditions of transformation of that space, always exists according to a *genealogy* which sometimes dates back to before the age of capitalism. (It should be noted that this criticism of the micro-economic theory of location is also quite valid for the Jena school's theory of 'central places'.)

We must therefore distinguish two cases:

(1) *The 'competitive' case* where a marginal capitalist sets up in a social space without modifying it to any significant degree. He competes indirectly with the other candidates by means of the price of land and accepts that he has to pay for this land at a price which assures him an average profit. This is the mechanism of the process we have analysed under the name of 'exogenous differential tribute', that of the simple reproduction of the socio-economic division of space.[8]

(2) *The 'monopoly' case* where a capitalist (or a group), generally in conjunction with the State apparatus, decides to modify the socio-economic division of space by means of his own investment. From then on only concerted action (at the political level of spatial planning) or if need be, economic hegemony, permits this 'extended reproduction-restructuring' of a social space which monopoly capital is assured of controlling through the mechanism of 'endogenous differential tribute'.

It will be seen that only the first case is analogous with the mechanism of the law of value operating in competitive commercial exchange, except that the structure of space is a presupposition of the working of this mechanism since the reallocation of social capital between the different branches was the *result* of the functioning of the law of value.

In the second case only concerted action or public initiative can make up for the absence of a purely economic regulator of the restructuring of space. The ACRES study of the tertiary centre of Part-Dieu, with the part played there by the first offices to be set up and particularly the commercial centre which was fitted into the pre-existing Lyons framework, shows how difficult the problem is. Similarly, comparison between the mechanism of organic development of the port of Marseilles and the creation from scratch of the port of Fos shows the difference in forms of spatial development between competitive capital and monopoly capital.

We must insist on a second fundamental difference between the regulatory mechanisms of the appropriation of land and the law of value. In capitalist commercial exchange the autonomous sections of capital exchange values (commodities or money) between themselves. In the competition for occupation of land, capitalists pay *the owners of land* a *tribute* for the right of use of the land. Capitalist logic finds in this a foreign element: legal ownership which relates to an earlier use, which may well be pre-capitalist (small agricultural production), archaeo-capitalist (small and medium-sized enterprises) or extra-capitalist (housing). This situation can seriously upset capitalist spatial development by allowing a non-capitalist to benefit from the externalities resulting from public or private investment.

The Role of the State

The reflections above make it possible to specify two lines of State intervention:

(1) to make up for the lack of a 'law of value in space'. Essentially, this is the part it plays in spatial planning and initiatives in the restructuring of socio-economic space. It should be noted that, from the point of view of strict 'aspatial' economics, this role is further reinforced by the great cost of investments in spatial development (various lines and networks, port installations, etc.). If these investments were to function as capital, seeking an average rate of profit, the result would be such pressure on the mechanisms of equalisation of the rate of profit that they would never be undertaken.
(2) To impose capitalist logic on the inadequate framework of legal space. This role is performed through various mechanisms, from expropriation (which purely and simply cancels the legal rights protecting the earlier use of the land) to procedures such as Zones d'Aménagement Différé (ZAD) (which prevent landowners from benefiting from the endogenous differential tribute engendered by infrastructural development activities). Thus the BERU study on Dunkirk shows how the power of public institutions is directly employed as a legal agent in the restructuring of a pre- or palaeo-capitalist space by monopoly private capital (Usinor).[9]

Conclusion

The analysis which concludes the previous section assigns a double role to the State, as far as the spatial forms of capitalist development are concerned. The first (making up for the lack of a 'law of value in space') refers to the inability of private capital alone to assure the regulation of its own extended spatial development. It involves essentially the economic character of spatial policy. The second (to remove the legal obstacles placed by former landowners in the way of the logic of advanced forms of capitalist development) refers to the coexistence, with these advanced economic forms, of other stages and modes of production in the social formation: this is the politico-legal character of spatial policy.

Fundamentally, the question refers to nothing less than the proper role of the political instance in any social formation. According to Poulantzas[10] the political instance is that in which the unity of the social formation is reflected and reproduced. In social formations which appear as an articulation of several modes of production, under the domination of one of them, the functions of the institutions and centres of political power will therefore be:

(1) to bring about conditions (economic, political, ideological) for the reproduction (eventually extended . . . or brought to an end) of each of the modes, provided that the conditions of such reproduction are not totally included in the economic instance;
(2) to intervene in order to speed up, slow down or reverse the processes of articulation of the modes of production coexisting in the formation.

We have just seen the implications of these general imperatives as far as spatial policy is concerned. The case is much the same at a more macro-sociological level, the level of regional action. Faced with the uneven development of socio-economic regions, the State must take care to avoid sparking off the political or social struggles which would arise from too abrupt a dissolution or integration of archaic modes of production. This is what it does in a general fashion when it inhibits the process of articulation (protectionism) or when it intervenes promptly to remove social consequences (permanent displacement allowances). But as soon as internal and international evolution make it necessary, capitalist development assigns to the State the role of controlling and encouraging the establishment of a new inter-regional division of labour. This 'projected space' comes into more or less violent conflict with 'inherited space'. State intervention must therefore take the form of organising the substitution of projected space for present space, which implies:

political interventions which are a compromise with the peripheral, local dominant social groups;

political and social interventions in regard to local dominated classes;

modifications of legal space (ZAD, declaration of public utility, etc.);

technical-economic interventions (infrastructure).

So we reach the most general case of the *production of territorial space*, now emphasising that it also involves the destruction of the earlier social space through adjustments which must be analysed case by case. There can be no doubt that this is how to understand the contrast between 'land logic' and 'industrial logic' drawn by the Système d'Etude des Schémas d'Aménagement.

Notes

1. Spatiality translates the French *spatialité* coined by Lipietz as the geographical equivalent of the historical temporalities of the different instances of modes of production – eds.

2. For elaboration of this point see F. Perroux, *L'Economie du XXème Siecle* (Presses Universitaires de France, Paris, 1964).

3. The outline was developed by P.P. Rey in his book *Les Alliances des Classes* (Maspero, Paris, 1973) with the aim of dealing with the classical articulation of the capitalist and feudal modes of production.

4. This concept is put forward in S. Amin's book *Unequal Development* (Harvester Press, Lewes, Sussex, 1976).

5. See R. Vernon, *Sovereignty at Bay* (Basic Books, New York, 1971).

6. For a fuller discussion concerning the Lyons metropolis see ACRES, *Creation d'un Centre Tertiaire dans une Métropole Regionale* (Atelier Co-opératif de Recherches Economiques et Sociales, Paris, 1974).

7. For an example of the attempt to constitute a 'micro-economics in space' see W. Alonso, 'A Reformulation of Classical Location Theory and its Relation to Rent Theory', *Papers of the Regional Science Association* (1967), pp. 23-44. For a consideration of some of the difficulties which arise in such an attempt see E. Von Böventer, *Théorie de L'Equilibre en Economie Spatiale* (Gauthier-Villars, Paris, 1962) and also T.C. Koopmans and M. Beckman, 'Assignment Problems and the Location of Economic Activity', *Econometrica*, vol. 25 (1957), pp. 63-76.

8. This is further explained in A. Lipietz, *Le Tribut Foncier Urbain* (Maspero, Paris, 1974).

9. See BERU, *Dunkerque: Changement Economique et Problème Foncier* (Bureau d'Etudes et de Recherches Urbaines, Paris, 1973).

10. See N. Poulantzas, *Political Power and Social Classes* (New Left Books, London, 1973).

THE REGIONAL FRAMEWORK OF MONOPOLY EXPLOITATION: NEW PROBLEMS AND TRENDS

Felix Damette

General Trends in Industrial Location

We intend to explain new trends appearing in the field of the location of industry in capitalist economies.

The dominant feature of the capitalist economies at the crisis stage of State Monopoly Capitalism in their increasing integration, in various forms, in world competition which is constantly becoming more severe. This strengthens all the factors contributing towards the reduction of rates of profit and it correspondingly emphasises the need for the monopolies and their State to mobilise all the means at their disposal to face up to this situation; but equally it leads them to seek new means, which deserve to be analysed in greater depth.

Contradictions of Surplus Profit

At the level of the firm, one of the means of combating the tendency towards the reduction of the rate of profit is to make a surplus profit. For a given enterprise surplus profit arises from advantages in comparison to its principal competitors which can be, in their essentials, any of the following: a technical advance, a more favourable geographical location, greater exploitation of the labour force.

The present conditions of monopoly finance, the centralisation of capital and State intervention, tend to speed up the rate of investment and of convergence of the level of technology between monopolies. The life expectancy of a technical advance is reduced when its cost rises. In the context of the take-off of the scientific and technical revolution, new techniques require massive investments, but the surplus profits which they permit are immediately threatened as a result of international competition. This is one of the causes of monopolistic accumulation and over-accumulation. The result is a process by which monopolies' technology converges, which sharply reduces the technical basis for making a surplus profit.

On the question of location, the development of transport produces an identical result, by greatly reducing the returns arising from geographical advantages. Indeed, the element of transport costs in prices tends to fall, which is related to a certain extent to a process of relative equalisation of locations, provided of course that they are served by suitable means of transport. But distance alone has only secondary importance compared with accessibility. This process of equalisation of locations is complex, and results from the convergence of several factors. In the field of shipping, technical developments have played a decisive role. The reduction of costs per tonne carried is important and tends to reduce inter-continental distances considerably. In the field of surface transport, operating conditions work in the same way. Shared between the public sector and small and middle-sized enterprises, this is an area of heavy devalorisation, making a transfer to the profit of the monopolies by operating with reduced tariffs. For these structural reasons transport costs are reduced; their part in the cost of the final product is diminished and hence their part in locational rent. From the moment when communications infrastructure is established, the situation of an enterprise at such and such a point of the network has only secondary importance.

Thus the technical and geographical foundations for making surplus profit tend to be reduced as the importance of such profit to monopolies is increasing. From this it can be seen that human elements play the essential role, that is the increased exploitation of labour power. The production of surplus profit is increasingly linked to super-exploitation.

The Problems of Super-exploitation

The increasing importance of super-exploitation comes into direct contradiction with the crisis of capitalist exploitation, particularly in areas of dense concentration of labour. From this arises the increased tendency to seek 'reserves' of labour which provide big capital with conditions for the super-exploitation of workers.

These particular conditions arise in three very different spheres.

At the international scale: (1) underdeveloped, politically dominated countries which possess a minimal infrastructure offer optimal conditions to monopolies. Big capital finds the employment of this labour there clearly preferable to immigration which necessarily brings the level of wages into line with those of the host country. This tendency is bound to grow considerably stronger, with all that this implies as regards 'co-operation', that is associated measures for a policy of neo-colonialist investment.

At the national scale, reserves of labour exist, at low relative cost: (2) in all agricultural regions, and especially in areas of high population growth such as Western France; (3) in the heavily underemployed female population. In practice the two factors are connected, and research is in progress into the question of female labour in agricultural regions.

These trends have existed for some years, but they become more pervasive with the crisis of State Monopoly Capitalism. The 'redeployment' proposed by employers and those in power means basically a series of conversions directed towards external markets, closely associated with changes of location with a view to seeking 'reserves' of lower-cost labour.

The truth is that the geographical conditions which allow super-exploitation represent untapped sources of profit which capital will exploit as soon as these conditions exist. By definition it is an unstable system, constantly seeking new areas and always ready to abandon those sectors which lose their relative 'interest'.

In the present context of France this induces different crisis situations depending on the region. While industrial regions like the Paris region, Nord, Rhône- Alpes, suffer mass dismissals, mixed or predominantly agricultural regions (West, Paris Basin) can face complex situations with dismissals at certain points but also the creation of unskilled and underpaid jobs at others; 'decentralisations' are highly likely to increase these.

On the whole, geographical conditions of production become increasingly important, not from the classic angle of national wealth or ease of communication, but from the fact of the primary role played by regional factors in the conditions of super-exploitation of workers.

The So-called Spatial Policy

The central problem in spatial planning is to offer monopolies the optimal spatial conditions for maximising profits. The problem is to create the most 'favourable' conditions for settlement of both industry and services. We have seen that 'regional' factors have become increasingly involved in the problem of monopolies and that this trend could only become more marked with the crisis.

This leads the State to broaden and, at the same time, to refine its intervention. In fact a diversification of actions can be observed, tending to integrate the whole territory, and also a parallel concentration of decisions, on one hand at the level of the Prefects of regions, on the other at the central level. The integration of DATAR (Délégation à l'Aménagement du Territoire et à l'Action Regionale) into the Ministère de l'Equipment is only one aspect of this process.

But the capitalist system comes up against a major contradiction over the question of industrial location policy. The principal tendency of monopolies is towards geographical concentration. Their immediate concern is in fact to gather together labour power in order to facilitate recruitment, flexibility and mobility. The convenience of large pools of labour with a range of skills is obvious; it makes it possible to set up new establishments or to modify existing production without seriously having to worry about problems of training. The size of the labour market determines a 'flexibility effect' for the enterprise. In this, geographical concentration is an essential factor.

However, in the longer term, concentration leads to an increase in the cost of labour power, first by its direct urban effects; by the effect of massing populations in urban areas and in particular through rent mechanisms, the large city involves higher transport and accommodation costs which have powerful repercussions on the cost of labour power. Costs of labour power are also increased by the indirect social effects of concentration and in the first place raising the level of consciousness and militancy of workers in large centres. At the same time the diversity and size of enterprises in a large town create conditions for competition between firms. Such competition is relatively favourable for the workers.

During a boom period the favourable aspects of concentration weigh more heavily with monopolies, which are anxious to find the necessary labour quickly, even at the price of higher wage costs. In actual fact, the trend towards the concentration of labour came out on top in the power politics which accompanied the boom period of State Monopoly Capitalism, with the policy of métropoles d'équilibre and with the Paris policy put forward by the Schéma Directeur of 1965.

During a period of recession the unfavourable aspects for monopolies came to the fore and this leads the State to seek new solutions to this contradiction: a new form of concentration of labour in regroupment areas which are both specialised and diffuse at the same time.

The basic element is the 'labour reserve'. It is organised towards:

(1) *Specialisation*: the uniformity of the skill structure enables monopolies to tell in advance what recruitment prospects in the area will be like; at the same time it limits competition between firms and enables them to fix wages at the lowest level, with a certain reserve of unemployment. This assumes that firms are organised in very specialised units in order to utilise this uniform structure.

(2) *Diffusion*: these reserves are intended to avoid the spatial consolidation characteristic of urban agglomerations. Through urban policy and housing policy they aim to achieve a spread of labour in small

towns and the countryside surrounding the principal centre of employment. Fashionable ideas on 'the environment' came just at the right moment to provide an ideological cloak for the system. Medium-sized towns, the human scale, the quality of life, nature, etc., are invoked to dress it up.

(3) This policy of specialised concentration goes hand in hand with the *hierarchical organisation* of regroupment areas, which takes effect on the national scale at three levels:

(i) basic labour reserves are organised round medium-sized towns, and are relevant to the majority of labour-intensive industries;
(ii) large towns concentrate more complex industries and ordinary services intended for the basic reserves;
(iii) the Paris region is primarily the headquarters of State Monopoly Capital, which is trying to make it a business capital on the European scale. Under such pressure, the contradictions take an acute turn.

The Basic Reserves

The use of these reserves, which started some years ago, will become generalised and systematised in the context of the crisis of State monopoly capital, thanks in particular to the so-called medium-sized towns policy. This especially affects industrial labour and in particular both male and female semi-skilled workers. The problem is to provide, from the resources of a town and its surrounding rural area, the several thousand semi-skilled workers needed by industry. But the same problem arises from highly concentrated heavy industries like steel-making. Dunkirk is a good example.

In general, these reserves are organised round an urban centre, within a radius equal to the daily maximum commuting distance by motor transport. They should be situated at a convenient distance from a large industrial centre; in practice this means within 250 to 350 km, a distance which allows a lorry to make the return trip within a day; motorways play a fundamental part in this.

State intervention develops at this level both under the guise of the 'medium-sized towns' policy and through rural development; one of the essential elements is the inducement and coercion of local authorities, to get them to increase their revenues in order to set up the structure for dealing with an influx of newcomers. There are in fact at this level relative 'reserves' of local tax revenue which allow development at least cost to the monopolies and the State. Since the establishments involved are relatively light, the infrastructural costs are quite limited. State intervention is therefore essentially political; one of the delicate problems raised by this operation is that of the relationship with the middle classes, especially small and medium-sized enterprises. It is they who must in part bear the fiscal consequences of the operation, while some of them run the risk of being eliminated or dominated by the mere fact of the arrival of the monopolies. The situation in these circumstances is complicated, however, depending on the extent to which certain categories (building, services) can hope to integrate themselves into the system and profit from this form of growth. Here there is room for the State and the monopolies to manoeuvre, which they are not slow to make use of, both at the local level and increasingly at the regional scale.

Métropoles d'Equilibre

These go back to an older policy which can be evaluated. It relates only to a limited number of towns: about half a dozen. Their principal role is to concentrate regional investment and the common services for different basic labour reserves. We have seen in fact a fairly large growth of tertiary employment; correspondingly industry has developed with a withdrawal of big establishments outside large towns.

Politically the weight of State supervision is more heavily felt; the local bourgeoisies, often represented by more or less centrist municipalities, have a base in commerce, land and property, and less and less in industry. They follow in the footsteps of changes of power, while trying to gain the greatest possible advantage from them.

Urban policy is characterised by the priority given to road transport infrastructure to serve centres, which none the less remain weak and where redevelopment is limited to offices and prestige operations. This leads to a political impasse, in particular with the indebtedness of local authorities and increased weight of local taxation. This is where the new regional tax system will come to the aid of urban budgets in difficulties. A political battle takes place between the agents of the State and those of the local bourgeoisie; we saw their ups and downs while the 'regions' in 'Haute Normandie' and 'Rhône-Alpes' were being set up. Obviously this struggle is not fundamental, but it does indicate actual tensions.

The Paris Region

The enormous edifice of the Paris region suffers most from the crisis of State Monopoly Capitalism. The impetus comes from the bureaucratisation of the system, in the political field as much as the economic. This brings about the creation of a massive number of office jobs, and intense speculation in land and property.

To try to limit the effects of this growth, the State exerts severe pressure on labour-intensive industries to induce them to move out to the provinces. This brings on a social crisis, particularly for the working class, and an urban crisis since the result is a monstrous concentration of jobs in an already saturated centre, in which the transport system reaches the verge of complete paralysis. Commuter journeys become longer and longer. The new pseudo-towns launched during the boom period of State Monopoly Capitalism are reduced to huge, very expensive, suburbs, even more unbalanced than the rest. The inner suburbs deteriorate; the balance of employment is lost; local communities are placed in untenable positions.

It is here that the authoritarianism of the State reaches its highest proportions. The State decides the general outline directly without consulting any intermediaries of a local bourgeoisie. The contradictions of the system have reached their highest level in the Paris region. This region is the focus of the general crisis of the system, where the worker's living conditions are most intolerable. The crisis of State Monopoly Capitalism has its strongest effect there. Collective dismissals increase in industry, while the State is led to put pressure on certain parts of the 'tertiary' sector to induce them in turn to move out to the provinces. This action is obviously selective and, as in the case of industry, consists of trying to clear the 'semi-skilled workers of the tertiary sector' out of Paris so as to reinforce the concentration of activities directly connected with the central management of capitalism.

Fundamentally, this is the result of the policy of 'hierarchical organisation' discussed earlier. It can only strengthen the internal and external factors of exploitation.

The Conditions of the Geographical Adjustment of Monopolistic Institutions to Economic Change[1]

We have seen the general trends of industrial location; it remains to identify how monopolies adjust to these new conditions.

The logic of profit leads to a generalised instability of production, from the sectoral and geographical point of view. The rule is the 'displacement' of capital in the joint search for a sectoral 'loophole', which by its very definition is ephemeral, and for a reserve of cheaper labour. The spatial field of this instability lies at two different scales.

On the international plane: the export of capital is impelled both by the 'attractive' measures of certain States and also by the policy of encouragement practised by the French State. This causes a double movement: on the one hand, the establishment of industries with a high organic composition of capital in developed countries which offer an important market; on the other hand, the establishment of labour-intensive industries in dominated underdeveloped countries with a large reserve of population.

On the national plane: in France itself the problem of location is put in different terms according to whether the investment is made by an enterprise which is not yet established in the country or by an existing firm (French or foreign). In the first case we observe either the purchase and 'restructuring' of a medium-sized French firm, or the creation of a new one; in most cases these firms set up 'branch' plants with a relatively low organic composition of capital; they make full use of the financial facilities offered by the French State, preferring to settle in 'assisted' zones, that is in general predominantly agricultural areas or areas undergoing an acute crisis.

For enterprises already established in France, the problem is different and is generally presented in terms of a choice between the expansion or modification of an existing establishment or the creation of an establishment on a new site. This kind of problem depends on simple economic calculations familiar to businesses.

The 'expansion *in situ*' solution is generally simpler and cheaper: the enterprise finds it more tempting since it makes operation easier; it simplifies problems of inter-departmental relations, staffing and management.

The 'relocation' solution can avoid putting a strain on the labour market of the existing establishment and enables firms to find clear sites; above all it best suits the 'current' requirements of profit maximisation by selecting the site best adapted to the new conditions of competition. The firm's previous sites correspond, by their very definition, to the 'out-of-date', quasi-historic conditions of another level of competition.

Obviously the concrete terms of the problem depend on a great number of factors, on technical conditions of production, the size of the proposed operation, the firm's own strategy, etc.

The Effect of the Mechanisms of State Monopoly Capitalism on Location Problems

Basically, the movement of enterprises is the result of the generalised instability of capital; geographical migrations are first of all the spatial resultant of sectoral shifts. But State Monopoly Capitalism intervenes equally through mechanisms whose effects are in fact spatial and which considerably strengthen tendencies to geographical instability.

On one hand, taxation procedures produce a false depreciation of existing establishments. All the mechanisms of accelerated depreciation, of super-amortisation, tend to speed up the rhythm of investment, but also seriously alter the figures used in economic calculations regarding location. The advantages of in-situ expansion are largely linked with the size of existing investment. Systematic depreciation falsifies the facts of the problem and weakens the trend towards 'linear' development of activities, or continuous evolution at existing locations.

At the same time the mechanisms of State Monopoly Capitalism tend to reduce the cost of new locations for enterprises. The State itself bears the cost of infrastructure and of part of the cost of major investments; in the framework of the so-called spatial planning policy, premiums, rebates on loans and tax relief are used to support and strengthen the tendency to set up on a new site. In addition, local communities become rivals to offer firms the most generous facilities for location.

In this way, the different procedures characteristic of State Monopoly Capitalism have the effect of seriously upsetting the rules of location by systematically favouring the tendency to 'removal and relocation', as opposed to the tendency to 'in-situ development'. The comparative costs of the two solutions no longer bear any relation to what they would be under a 'simple' monopoly system, without State intervention; the calculation in real costs to the enterprise no longer exists and is replaced by entirely artificial data; but this does not represent a shift towards a system of real communal costs, rather the contrary.

The system which emerges is even further removed from social interest than the previous ones, and represents a real institutionalisation of chaos. In fact the community bears a triple cost in this:

(1) The cost of installation is the most obvious but it is important to measure its real extent; socially it is not limited to the problem of industrial zones and their services; we must include the real long-term costs of incoherent urban development. The jerky rates of growth of such towns are in marked contrast to the mess represented by the excessive growth rates of Zones d'Implantation Préférentialles.

(2) The removal itself represents a social upheaval which is difficult

to measure. While the enterprise takes advantage of the operation to settle its staffing problems in its own way, leading to what amounts to a disguised lay-off and most often complete dismissal, the workers concerned are placed in extremely serious positions which often lead them to sacrifice family ties, their spouses' jobs or their own jobs.

(3) The cost of moving out rises to unimaginable proportions in areas heavily affected by recession. Who can count the real cost to the community of the destruction of the mining areas of Nord or the Lorrainese uplands? What are the consequences of the damage caused by the frantic de-industrialisation of the Paris region? These are the real spatial policy problems.

At all events, it can be affirmed that State Monopoly Capitalism has succeeded in establishing the most expensive possible geographical mode of expansion while multiplying confusion at every stage of the proceedings (to mention only the spatial dimension of the problem).

By doing away with the economic and spatial regulation of classical capitalism to the advantage of the monopolies, State Monopoly Capitalism does not in any way arrive at a superior rationality. On the contrary, it arrives at a whole range of deeper contradictions, whose temporary solution implies increasing intervention on the part of the State, and henceforth of local authorities, at a higher and higher social cost.

Thus one becomes aware of a geographical instability of capital which is the direct consequence of its structural instability; but to this can be added an instability which is strictly speaking spatial, arising from the mechanisms of State Monopoly Capitalism, and which overlaps the field of the first. This is why one can conclude that the most important laws of the organisation of space under State Monopoly Capitalism are the result of the *hypermobility of capital*.

In fact there is a process of accelerated obsolescence of industrial sites; the changing character of the market and of competition brings about the rapid development of sites corresponding to the optimal location in terms of profit maximisation. It would be in the monopolies' interest to 'follow' the evolution of the market and constantly to adapt their locations, provided, of course, that this did not entail prohibitive costs for the firm itself and considerable social damage.

State Monopoly Capitalism has the power unilaterally to favour the monopolies' tendency to relocation by 'removing', through the intervention of public funds, the factors which promote the stability of enterprises and by allowing local communities and populations to suffer the damage caused by these processes. Chaos is therefore an integral part of the system. The hypermobility of capital is a consequence of the general phenomena of over-accumulation and devalorisation, but it also has the effect of accelerating and accentuating them.

The main result of the process is obviously to cause the hyper-mobility of people. Excessive migrations, with their trail of regional, social and human damage, become general. The regional balance of population movements has only a very limited significance; what matters nowadays is expressed by the volume of movements in and out. A reduced net volume of migratory movements as in the Paris region conceals an increase in immigration and especially in emigration. A hotch-potch of age brackets, levels of qualification, of professional categories is constantly generalised to adjust the labour market to the changing needs of monopoly profit. This displacement of people reaches such proportions and such importance that it can be considered today not only a condition but also as one of the elements of capitalist exploitation and it must be recognised as such (in all its aspects) by the labour movement.

The impact which certain regionalist claims have occasionally had among certain groups of young people arises basically from a perfectly legitimate rejection of this hypermobility imposed on people by the system. The regional dimension of the right to work is a demand which must be expressed in quantitative and qualitative terms; it will be made to an increasing extent.[2]

Some Examples of the Hypermobility of Capital

The most striking examples are found at the international level. Analysis of each monopoly would reveal this phenomenon, whether it involves the European strategy of Saint-Gobain-Pont-à-Mousson or better still the world strategy of Péchiney 'deployed' from the United States to Australia, from Guinea to the Netherlands whilst reducing its activities in France.

· Within the framework of this analysis we will confine ourselves to some national examples.

Plastics Manufacture

A decade ago production of polyethylenes depended to a large extent on the coal by-products industry, and an important centre was located at Mazingarbe (Pas-de-Calais). The system was a model of the operation of State Monopoly Capitalism. The basic unit consisted of the Houillères Nationales mines, which provided the crude product. This was supplied cheaply to the two immediately adjacent private factories of Ethylène-Plastique and Ethy-Synthèse which turned out the commercial product and pocketed the profit without having to make the principal investment.

But imperialist energy politics make petroleum a source of better returns for monopolies: Ugine-Kuhlmann closes its Mazingarbe factory and sets up again in the Basse-Seine area, converting to petrochemicals. The collieries have to cease production. Certainly it was perfectly logical for the monopolies concerned to want to change technique and location, bearing in mind the relative prices levels of coal and oil, which are themselves largely determined by power politics.

But they were unable to carry out this operation except with the active assistance of the State, which organised the ultra-rapid writing off of the coal by-products units, making possible their immediate closure as soon as the price levels altered; which allowed the closure of factories with the Houillères mine first of all, leaving the workers to sort out the cumulative effects of abandoned industry, mining recession, etc.; and which organised the new locations and strongly supported the development policy of the oil and chemicals monopolies, while leaving the consequences of the accelerated growth of the Basse Seine area for the local communities to deal with.

Thus on one side the result is the abandonment of activity in Nord, a region in which infrastructure is already underutilised, where houses stand empty, and on the other, a new concentration in the Basse-Seine area, which of all provincial regions is the one in which the cost of urban growth is highest. Without being able to measure the total cost of the operation, one can establish that in order to offer optimal conditions for profit to the petrochemical trusts, the State manages a double regional crisis, one of departure and one of arrival.

What was the cost to the State, the communities and the workers of the extra profit made in this way by Péchiney-Ugine-Kuhlmann and used by them to finance . . . their foreign investments? At all events, it can be affirmed that the true national interest is the loser all along the line.

Steel-making

This sector offers the best examples of the hypermobility of capital, to the extent that the migration of production is the rule, without even being linked to a change of technique as in the preceding example.

Great stress has been laid on the role of ores imported cheaply, thanks to the development of shipping techniques. This ignores the fact that the price of imported ore landed in France is very comparable with that of minette ore processed in Lorraine. It also ignores the role of imperialism in the fixing of the price of Mauritanian ore.

In fact, the strategy of the steel monopolies, orchestrated by some banking groups, is revealed on the one hand by the abandonment of part of the French market to firms from Germany, Luxembourg and Belgium (with which the same banks are clearly connected) and on the other by the use of French State subsidies to create a coastal steel industry which is essentially directed towards exports.

It is quite ironic to note that at the very moment great claims are being made for the superiority of coastal steel-making over production on a landlocked site, the French market is being taken over more and more by foreign land-based steel industries (Belgium, Luxembourg, the Saar) which according to this fine scheme should be at the greatest disadvantage.

It is remarkable to see that the enormous transfer of public funds which has taken place in France to the profit of steel monopolies results in the retreat of these firms from the French market itself in the face of 'foreign' competition. We are in fact witnessing the use of different 'national' policies of devalorisation of capital by industrial finance groups on a supranational scale, which are able to work out a transnational strategy on this foundation. In concrete terms, this is shown by gigantic geographical transfers, Valenciennes to Dunkirk and Lorraine to Fos.

The State has done its utmost to provide Usinor and De Wendel with optimal conditions for entering external markets. It is obviously in the interest of the two or three banks controlling the operation (in particular Paribas and Suez), which also transnationalise themselves and carry out massive exports of capital.

That is why the State has not a moment's hesitation before destroying the Lorraine and Valenciennes steel industry, almost giving away infrastructure *in situ*, forcing Lorraine workers to go to work in the Saar. Meanwhile on the coast at Dunkirk and Fos urban and human imbalances increase, pulling in considerable quantities of labour from a great distance, and swallowing up enormous public credits, and particularly those of local authorities. This is where chaos reaches monumental proportions.[3]

The themes of technical progress and growth are feeble technocratic alibis, chorused by the government's blind supporters to make acceptable these purely monopolistic operations, whose real cost to the nation is incomparably greater than the resulting extra profit that the monopolies make and which they will use to set themselves up in Brazil or somewhere else.

This institutionalisation of chaos is only possible through the generalised intervention of the State, which acts in all fields and at all levels to clear 'obstacles' to the maximisation of monopoly profit within the framework of world competition, whatever the real costs of these measures. It is clear that the basic problem is not location but the logic of monopoly profit and the objective limits which it has reached.

There would appear to be no solution to the problems of the steel industry except complete nationalisation, which is a *sine qua non* of a reorientation on the basis of the development of the national market and the optimal use of existing infrastructure and installations. This would allow faster growth of production, and at the same time a reduction in the real social cost of that growth, by a massive reduction in direct and indirect costs, by clearing up the muddles which are multiplied at present.

On the whole the mechanisms of growth developed by State Monopoly Capitalism are revealed by distortions, which can become grotesque, between the logic of monopoly profit and a completely coherent policy of social development. In particular, State intervention engenders hypermobility of capital, which leads to the most expensive possible type of growth to the community. Nowadays it is the rule to scrap infrastructure, to underutilise or abandon parts of certain sectors, while elsewhere new infrastructure is being created at great public expense. Generalised instability becomes predominant.

The crisis of State Monopoly Capitalism accelerates these processes and requires in its turn a more emphatic, more systematic State intervention aimed at the generalised authoritarian control of all parts of the country, of all forms of finance, to push devalorisation procedures to the extreme in order to strengthen the machinery of exploitation and super-exploitation of the workers.

The Spatial Dimension of State Intervention

Spatial policy is only one and probably not the most important aspect of State intervention in the question of organisation of space.

The central function of the State is to organise the devalorisation of capital so as to adapt it still better to the requirements of monopoly profit in a fluctuating and constantly more difficult context. To do this, the channels of devalorisation are multiplied, the procedures diversified.

Taxation and subsidy by the nationalised sector represent two constant and regular channels. To these can be added public-sector markets, agreements and plans, and above all the direct intervention of the State to create the infrastructure necessary for the development of monopoly capital. The case of the industrial and port bases is the best known; one can add the big urban operations (La Défense, located in Paris) and regional tourist developments (Languedoc).

In general State intervention is not confined to the strictly defined sphere of production. Public capital comes into play to set up an 'environment' necessary for profitable production.

Indirect Devalorisation

Public capital is not only the devalorised capital discussed in the preceding paragraphs, it is also the whole of the 'social capital' needed by the population as well as production. Very important sectors are concerned: public health installations; training establishments; urban facilities; motorways; telecommunications; 'social' housing; etc.

It involves elements which make an important contribution to monopoly profit but which are not directly involved in this monopoly profit, both on account of their content and because of the channels of decision-making and finance. From the point of view of content, these factors are expressed in terms of social needs and are claimed with more or less vigour by local people. From the operational point of view, local authorities have an important place in decision-making and finance.

One of the key problems of the current phase, which is also one of the most typical problems of State Monopoly Capitalism, is found at this level. Under the pressure of world competition, the system is forced to 'mobilise' investments in social capital towards monopoly profit. This is basically the result of the growing socialisation of productive forces, led astray by the profit system. In a way it is a matter of 'arranging' the general costs of facilities in order to transform them into devalorised capital at the service of monopoly profit. This objective, clearly expressed in the Ortoli-Montjoie report, has become the central question of the Plan.

Spatial Selectivity

To a certain extent it is a question of enlarging the sphere of the devalorisation of capital so as to include in it the maximum of public funds. The problem is to engage as directly as possible all the public interventions with the development of monopoly capital; to do that

one of the essential means is to obtain spatial selectivity so that operations take place not where the pressure of social needs is strongest but
where the development of monopoly capital requires it. This selectivity
implies a strict arrangement of communities by the combined action of
authoritarian administrative measures and the Plan. The Regional Plans
for Economic Development, the Infrastructure Modernisation Plans and
the regionalisation of the Plan in the hands of Prefects are the essential
tools in this field.

In this sense, local communities are in a key position in the arrangement. Not only is it imperative to have them economically and politically subordinate, but it is equally vital to have the 'participation' of
those concerned, certainly on the fiscal plane but also on the political
plane, if only to justify and rubber-stamp fiscal participation. In this
respect, the new regional organisation which has just been set up is a
model of its type.

Basically, the regime is led to the necessity of making the population 'participate' in what is in the long run its own exploitation. This is
quite typical of the crisis of State Monopoly Capitalism, of the political
battle now in progress and of the possibilities of rapid change which lie
hidden in the Programme Commun.

Conclusion

In the end the regime's spatial policies must be considered as a whole,
taking the information relating directly to spatial policy in the light of
the policy followed towards local communities, regional reforms, the
Plan, etc.

The overall policy constitutes a coherent whole; it aims at an organisation of space which is essentially a spatial organisation of capitalist
exploitation. Within the framework of world competition it means
optimising the use of potential sources of profit; in a deeper sense the
aim is to organise the country so as to place the workers in conditions which allow the maximum exploitation, internally within the enterprise and externally in society.

The specialised, hierarchical system which this represents implies
the generalisation of human mobility, both for inter-regional migration
and daily commuting. Different stages of life will be marked by
important migrations, with all that this involves in the way of personal
and family problems.

The question has to be asked: what is the meaning in this context
of the very concept of region? To be honest, it conceals a contradiction
which becomes glaring, between two processes acting in opposite direc-

tions.

Monopolistic concentration and the integration of the economy across national boundaries lead to an *accelerated de-regionalisation of economic relationships*. In the majority of cases regional structures are a historical memory. The national structure itself is threatened. At this fundamental level the idea of region has already lost all real significance. The middle classes, bound to the regional structures of the past, are faced with the dilemma of elimination or integration with the monopolistic system.

Conversely, we are witnessing a process of *regionalisation of economic problems*, particularly of the central problem — that of exploitation. The system is led to refine its interventions, to take the local situation into account in order to optimise the conditions of exploitation. This concerns industrial location policy as much as policies for training and provision of facilities. Having been eliminated as an economic structure, the region reappears with another meaning and on a different scale, as the framework of exploitation. The channels of capitalist exploitation multiply and diversify with increasing State intervention. This is accompanied by a more vigorous adaptation to local conditions with the attempt to establish a complete co-ordinated system. The new regions which are emerging (unrelated to administrative or historical traditional divisions) are essentially characterised by a specific combination of different forms of exploitation: rural exodus, emigration, internal exploitation, fiscal pressure, living conditions, underdevelopment of public services.[4]

Ultimately the region can be defined not only as a framework but as a form of worker exploitation, taking these two terms in their broadest sense.

Notes

1. See J. Delilez, *Les Monopoles* (Editiones Sociales, Paris n.d.).

2. It is clear that the real solution lies in national policy and that the regionalist trap lies in framing a justifiable claim in a way which prevents the struggle from being conducted on its true ground and which lends itself to all the manoeuvres aimed at dividing workers and ensuring class collaboration at the regional level.

3. Damette's conclusions have been further confirmed by recent events in the French steel industry. In June 1979, the prestigious Fos project was in total disarray, with up to 5,000 redundancies in prospect. See *Le Monde*, 13-14 May 1979 – eds.

4. This question is discussed further in Chapter 5.

5 GLOBAL CRISIS AND REGIONAL CRISES

Felix Damette and Edmond Poncet

The capitalist system is undergoing a deep, lasting, structural crisis. At the same time the existence of more or less acute regional crises is evident. The purpose of this study is to examine the relationship between these two levels of crisis, starting from a double working hypothesis:

Regional crises ultimately reflect the general crisis of the system. The initial force is provided by the general crisis.
Regional crises are not the result of simple disaggregation of the overall crisis. There is a specifically regional dimension to the problem.

This double hypothesis will determine our approach; essentially it consists of distinguishing the boom period of State Monopoly Capitalism, roughly the sixties, from the period of global crisis over the last few years. We will attempt to define the chief characteristics of the different regional crises which occurred in the course of the boom period so that we can then turn to the problem of their development in the crisis phase of State Monopoly Capitalism.

To do this, we intend to adopt a descriptive procedure while seeking above all to establish a typology. In fact, the information available at the regional scale scarcely permits a fundamental analysis at the theoretical level. There are hardly any regional economic statistics in France and the only complete and coherent figures available concern population and employment. For this reason we intend to tackle regional problems from the angle of employment and the labour market; it should, however, be clearly understood that this is a partial approach which does not allow one to go much beyond the descriptive level. (See the methodological discussion and definition of terms in the Appendix.)

The Balance-sheet of the Boom Period (1962-68)

Overall Results

For the period 1962-8 at the national level the number of young people reaching working age was 2.3 million of each sex, that is, 4.6 million. But whereas almost the entire male section comes on to the labour market, only a little more than half the women do so, say 1.2 million. The effective demand for jobs from young people is about 3.5 million. Against this, the demographic outflow is about 3 million (2,100,000 men and 900,000 women). On this basis, some half a million new jobs are needed (of which 200,000 should be for men and 300,000 for women).

In fact the problem is different because the demographic flow cuts across the economic flow. It is as though a third of the available jobs, 950,000 to be more precise, had been scrapped. At the same time, however, 1.85 million new jobs were created. Let us take the balance sheet as shown in Table 5.1.

Table 5.1: Employment Balance-Sheet, 1962-68

Effective Demand for Labour		Labour Supply	
Jobs available	3,000,000	Young people (French)	3,500,000
Jobs scrapped	950,000	Immigrants (young people and adults)	650,000
Jobs left	2,050,000		
New jobs	1,850,000		4,150,000
Jobs effectively available	3,900,000		

This leaves a *balance of 250,000 people*, corresponding to the number of people made unemployed during the period.

There are several general points to be noted:

(1) the importance of the creation of jobs during the period;
(2) the importance of jobs created in relation to newcomers arriving on the labour market: new jobs almost equal 'traditional' jobs (47 per cent as against 53 per cent);
(3) the high level of underemployment of women: more than a million (over six years);
(4) but this situation is changing and the demand for new employment is greater for women (300,000) than for men (200,000). There is therefore an element of compensation, still moderate at the time in question but tending to accelerate;
(5) the relatively high level of unemployment creation, equivalent to

6 per cent of the total inflow (young people plus immigrants).

The Growth of Employment

For the period 1962-8, the surplus of employment is about 900,000; it represents the balance between 1.85 million jobs created and 950,000 jobs lost — chiefly in agriculture and mining. This balance of 900,000 is divided between 550,000 for men and 350,000 for women. The structure of jobs created is very different for the two sexes; public administration is responsible for 13 per cent of new male jobs but for 38 per cent of those for women. The strong influence and the special role of the State represent the prime features of female employment to-day.

Overall, jobs created between 1962 and 1968 account for 10.3 per cent of the stock existing in 1962, losses for 5.5 per cent and the balance 4.8 per cent. However, there are considerable regional variations. The balance ranged from + 12.2 per cent in Provence-Côte d'Azur to - 3.2 per cent in Limousin. It is possible to distinguish the following types:

(1) Regions of high growth (job creation above the national average; few losses): Haute-Normandie, Picardie, Champagne-Ardennes, Rhône-Alpes, Franche-Comté. In these regions it is industry which has provided the driving force except in Rhône-Alpes, where growth has chiefly been in the tertiary sector.

(2) Regions of low growth (job creation equal to or lower than the national average; losses much higher): Basse-Normandie, Pays de la Loire, Bourgogne, Poitou-Charentes, Aquitaine, Auvergne, Midi-Pyrénées, Bretagne. These are areas with a large peasant population which have suffered a severe reduction in agricultural employment. The situation is particularly bad in the Aquitaine-Midi-Pyrénées-Auvergne group and in Bretagne.

(3) In addition to these two basic groups, a series of special cases may be distinguished:

    (i) Provence-Côte d'Azur which combines the highest job creation rate with the lowest loss rate.

    (ii) Languedoc-Roussillon and Centre have very high rates in both directions with a large positive balance. Actually the situations are very different since the Centre holds the record for industrial growth while Languedoc is practically last in this respect.

    (iii) The Paris region has a lower job creation rate than the national average (9 per cent) but a much lower loss rate (2.3 per cent), which results in a growth rate clearly higher than average, with nearly 30 per cent of the national balance of employment.

(iv) Alsace represents a case apart with low rates on both sides, that is a slight expansion but fairly strong resistance to employment loss by its traditional economy.

(v) Nord and Lorraine have a zero balance with losses making up for job creation.

(vi) Limousin is the only region to display a strong negative balance, with a low job creation rate (7 per cent) and the highest number of losses (10.3 per cent).

Thus there is a great diversity of situations from which we can pick out the following major features:

(1) The importance of mining and, especially, of agriculture in regional differentiation. While the majority of regions have identical rates of employment creation (15 regions come between 9 and 12 per cent), it is loss rates which make the difference (widely scattered between 2 and 10 per cent).

(2) The diversity of categories of growth. These can be summarised as follows: industrial in the Paris Basin and Franche-Comté; construction and public works in the West and Bourgogne; 'tertiary' in the South-West and Auvergne; tourism and construction in the Mediterranean zone; 'tertiary' with industrial decline in the Paris region; industrial decline in Nord and Lorraine; generalised weakness in Limousin; high balanced growth in Rhône-Alpes.

It should be noted that the only region in which there has been growth in different sectors is Rhône-Alpes and this is largely due to the considerable overall extent of growth there. The general rule is a 'specialisation' of growth which, if not unhealthy, can at least be considered suspect. In particular, the complete absence of any correlation between the growth of industrial employment and the growth of employment in services at the regional level certainly seems to be a distortion which is due to the logic of capitalist exploitation rather than to any choice by the region.

There is also regional distortion in the development of jobs for men and for women. The general female underemployment is aggravated by a very poor employment balance in several regions, in particular

Bretagne and Pays de la Loire, Midi-Pyrénées and Aquitaine, Franche-Comté and Rhône-Alpes. It should be emphasised that this phenomenon does not affect agricultural regions alone.

Growth and Needs

The reasoning which follows will bear exclusively on male employment for the sake of simplicity. Needs and growth will be evaluated solely in crude quantitative terms — the number of jobs needed and effectively created.

The parameters used are:

(1) The need for additional jobs: this is the difference between the number of young people in the region entering the labour market and the number of old people leaving it. This is a demographic parameter. Thus, on the national scale, 2.3 million young men enter the market, while 2.1 million old men leave it. Two hundred thousand extra jobs are therefore needed. If this is expressed as a percentage of the number of those leaving the market, a rate of 'need' of 10 per cent over six years is obtained.

(2) Supplementary jobs created: this is the difference between the number of jobs created and jobs lost during the period. For men, we have (in the major industrial branches) 1,215,000 jobs created and 665,000 lost. On this basis there is a balance of 550,000 supplementary jobs. Using the same base as before (the number of those leaving the labour market) we get a rate of 26 per cent.

During the period total male employment increased by 550,000. To meet this, employers and the State had at their disposal an internal demographic surplus of 200,000, and organised an external migration balance (French and foreign) of 475,000. If the number of people looking for employment totals 675,000, this is expressed in an increase in unemployment of 125,000.

At the regional level, the situations reveal extreme contrasts. Virtually no region corresponds to the national average. The contrasts are particularly marked demographically: the rates of supplementary jobs needed range from – 20 per cent for Limousin to + 55 per cent for Basse-Normandie; the Rhône-Alpes region alone is in the average position.

High positive rates (more than 10 per cent) are found to the west, north and east of the Paris Basin and in Franche-Comté. Average rates are found to the south of the Paris Basin, in Alsace, and to a certain

extent in the Nord area. In the Paris region there is a negative rate
(- 1.4 per cent). A large part of France is characterised by high negative
rates: Massif Central, South-West and the Mediterranean region. The
situation is particularly serious in Limousin (- 19.7 per cent) and Midi-
Pyrénées (- 15.5 per cent). In this vast area the normal demographic
renewal of the labour market is not working.

Against this, the rates of development of employment also show
great contrasts from the - 16 per cent of Lorraine, - 18 per cent of
Limousin to the + 61 per cent of Provence-Côte d'Azur. The main thing
to note is the regional concentration of the balance of jobs created (for
men). Out of a national total of 550,000 new jobs, 172,000 were in the
Paris region; 127,000 in the Paris Basin; 101,000 in the Mediterranean
region and 75,000 in the Rhône-Alpes region. Hence 86 per cent of the
total was located in these four areas.

The regional pattern can be summarised as follows:

(1) High growth of employment and demographic stagnation: Paris
region and Mediterranean region. One of the important features of the
French situation is that employment growth is found in crisis zones or
areas of demographic stagnation. The extreme is reached in Corsica
with an enormous growth quite unrelated to regional demography.
Without commenting on the economic content of this growth, one
can note the considerable disparity between the demographic and
economic development of these regions, which cannot fail to present
problems:

  (i) of internal and external migration — they have absorbed 60
      per cent of foreign immigrants;
 (ii) of infrastructure and public services — these regions have ex-
      perienced very harsh yet contrasted growth rates, under con-
      ditions disturbed by different forms of speculation. This is
      where the 'troubles' of capitalist growth reveal themselves
      most clearly; in a crisis of public facilities, public housing, etc.

(2) High growth of employment (rates of the order of 30 to 40 per
cent) and high demographic growth (rates of the order of 20 to 30
per cent). This involves the Paris Basin, Franche-Comté and to a
certain extent Rhône-Alpes, even though its demographic position is
clearly nearer the average (+ 10.5 per cent).

(3) Two regions, Alsace and Bourgogne, occupy a separate place,
with weak demographic rates (+ 6 per cent) and medium rates of
growth of employment (23 and 17 per cent).

(4) The four western regions stand out clearly with high demo-

graphic rates, always above the rates of growth of employment.
However, two cases of a quite different kind should be distinguished:

(i) Basse-Normandie (55 and 33 per cent) and Pays de la Loire (35
and 27 per cent) have high rates in some places with overall
only a moderate shortage of jobs, in particular for the Pays de
la Loire;

(ii) Bretagne (22 and 5 per cent) and Poitou-Charentes (22 and 3
per cent) are characterised on the other hand by a very important shortage due to the almost stagnant balance of employment (jobs created just make up for jobs lost).

(5) The South-West and the Massif Central (Aquitaine-Midi-Pyrénées-
Auvergne) are characterised by low or poor rates of growth of
employment (4 to 12 per cent) but also by a very depressed demographic situation (- 5 to - 15 per cent). These are areas with a serious
shortage of labour.

(6) Limousin must be taken separately; it combines a double demographic (- 19.7 per cent) and economic (- 17.9 per cent) fall in a
sort of equilibrium of catastrophe.

(7) Finally, Nord and Lorraine combine high demographic
growth (18.8 and 20.2 per cent) with a fall in employment, particularly marked in Lorraine (- 16 per cent).

Regional Crises during the Boom Period

This diversity of regional patterns makes it possible to establish a
'typology' of regional crises. Economic and demographic analysis of
the labour market shows up a certain number of fairly obvious imbalances. Three-quarters of the departments display a clear disparity
between the two rates, and whatever the content of economic growth
may be elsewhere, this disparity is in itself a sign of more or less pronounced imbalance which may go as far as a situation deserving the
term crisis. It should be understood that we are talking of regional
crises which at the time were linked with an overall situation of economic boom.

In relation to the mean rate of national demographic and economic
growth, it is possible to distinguish four broad types of situation, of
which two are obviously regional crisis situations, while one presents
complex problems.

(1) About 25 departments have favourable rates, with a demographic
expansion above or equal to the national average, and an economic

expansion above their demographic expansion. This characterises a
large part of the Paris Basin, Franche-Comté, the Northern Alps, the
Rhône and Gard valley. It should be noted that this represents a
continuous zone joining the valleys of the Rhône, the Seine and the
middle Loire. The Paris area extends towards the west as far as Caen,
to the south-west as far as Tours, towards the south-east as far as
Dijon where it meets the Rhône area (broadly defined), from Belfort
to the Côtières du Gard.

(2) A small number of departments present a special problem (high
positive economic growth rates, negative demographic rates). These
are the Paris region, the Alpes-Maritimes, Haute-Garonne, the
Rhône, Bouches-du-Rhône and l'Hérault. Obviously these are large
urban areas of vigorous growth. The economic rates are greater than
45 per cent while demographic rates are negative. It should be noted
that in this picture the Paris region is the least imbalanced, since it
can practically ensure the demographic renewal of its labour force,
which is not the case elsewhere. On this scale and using these criteria
it is not possible to describe this kind of imbalance in terms of crisis.
If there is a crisis it must be examined on a finer scale and with much
more precise criteria, in which case the question would no longer be
one of regional crisis but of urban crisis.

(3) About twenty important and heavily populated departments
have a demographic growth rate above, sometimes very much above,
the national average and in this context an employment growth rate
lower than they need. In this situation we can speak of regional
crisis. There is a clear employment deficit which has a direct bearing
on emigration and unemployment. We propose to call this situation
an 'active crisis' while distinguishing two variants. First *marked
active crisis*: high demographic growth (above the national average),
economic contraction (negative employment balance). This concerns
two types of region: mining (and frontier) regions – Moselle,
Meurthe et Moselle, Meuse, Ardennes, Pas-de-Calais; agricultural
regions – Bretagne and Poitou-Charentes (Côte-du-Nord, Morbihan
– Deux-Sèvres, Vienne-Charente). This type of crisis is obviously the
most serious. Second, simple active crisis: vigorous demographic and
positive but very inadequate economic growth. Nord appears
here as an industrial variant, but more often it is a question of crises
which are basically agricultural. This concerns two compact areas.
One is to the west, a band stretching from the Channel to Charente-
Maritime, across Basse-Normandie and the Pays de la Loire. The
other is to the east, the Haute-Marne-Haute-Savoie-Vosges group

(with, in this last case, an industrial dimension to the regional crisis).

Thus, overall, there are two large areas of active crisis: all of the West, the four planning regions (except Calvados and Finistère); the frontier zone stretching from the north-east of Pas-de-Calais to the Vosges with two complete regions, Nord and Lorraine, plus Aisne and Ardenne, Haute-Marne and Haute-Saône.

Demographers will not fail to notice that all this area forms part of France's 'fertile crescent'. We should add that it is also the area which has directly suffered damage resulting from European integration because of its economic structure: mining, steel, textiles and agriculture.

(4) Finally, there remains a vast compact block in the Centre and the South-East which shows rates clearly lower than the national average for both economic and population growth. This block extends from Cher to Ariège, from the Landes to Saône et Loire. The Pyrennean border and Puy-de-Dôme alone have satisfactory employment growth rates. The essential feature of these regions is that the population is being reduced by ageing. There is no renewal of the labour force. This is accompanied by stagnation or a more or less pronounced economic withdrawal.

We propose to describe this situation as '*subdued crisis*'. Here, also, two variants can be distinguished. First, a serious crisis which could be called '*completed*': this concerns areas of falling population and severe economic decline (employment growth rates lower than - 20 per cent). These are the zones which contribute to a negative migration balance and where the situation is catastrophic. They comprise a big central block stretching from Dordogne to Haute-Loire, covering Lot, Aveyron and Lozère and, to a certain extent, Cantal. As well as this block there are two zones of the same type: in the South-Gers and Ariège; in the Centre-Creuse and Indre. Second, *ordinary 'subdued' crisis*: employment rates are stable or falling moderately but in general they are higher than the demographic rates; in spite of their economic weakness these regions are importers of labour.

Ordinary 'subdued' crisis is characteristic of: Cher, Nièvre, Allier, Haute-Vienne, Corrèze, Landes, Lot-et-Garonne, Tarn, Tarn-et-Garonne, Aude and Ardèche. To a lesser degree, Loire and Saône-et-Loire, together with Finistère, could also be included.

Figure 5.1: French Departments

The Crisis Cycle

The different types of crisis represent a regular chain and one can speak of a real crisis cycle. In the case of continuous socio-economic evolution, based on the elimination of the peasantry, the situation progresses from active crisis to subdued and completed crisis by means of emigration and the progressive ageing of the population.

Five stages can be distinguished:

(1) simple active crisis (e.g. Orne-Mayenne or Haute-Saône);
(2) marked active crisis (e.g. Morbihan-Charente or Meuse), when employment growth rates are negative;
(3) subduing of the crisis: the beginning of ageing and reduction of the demographic growth rates (Finistère);
(4) subdued crisis: demographic growth rates fall to the level of or lower than employment rates (Tarn, Aude, Nièvre); this is a form of

KEY

1. Pas de Calais	30. Maine et Loire	60. Gironde
2. Nord	31. Sarthe	61. Lot et Garonne
3. Seine Maritime	32. Loire et Cher	62. Lot
4. Somme	33. Loiret	63. Cantal
5. Aisne	34. Yonne	64. Haute-Loire
6. Ardennes	35. Côte d'Or	65. Isère
7. Manche	36. Haute-Saône	66. Savoie
8. Calvados	37. Belfort	67. Landes
9. Eure	38. Vendée	68. Gers
10. Oise	39. Deux Sèvres	69. Tarn et Garonne
11. Marne	40. Vienne	70. Aveyron
12. Meuse	41. Indre et Loire	71. Lozère
13. Meurthe et Moselle	42. Indre	72. Ardèche
14. Moselle	43. Cher	73. Drôme
15. Bas Rhin	44. Nièvre	74. Hautes Alpes
16. Finistère	45. Saône et Loire	75. Basses Pyrénées
17. Côte du Nord	46. Jura	76. Hautes Pyrénées
18. Morbihan	47. Doubs	77. Haute Garonne
19. Ille et Vilaine	48. Charente Maritime	78. Tarn
20. Mayenne	49. Charente	79. Hérault
21. Orne	50. Haute-Vienne	80. Gard
22. Eure et Loir	51. Creuse	81. Vaucluse
23. Seine et Oise	52. Allier	82. Basses Alpes
24. Seine et Marne	53. Dordogne	83. Alpes Maritimes
25. Aube	54. Corrèze	84. Ariège
26. Haute-Marne	55. Puy de Dôme	85. Aude
27. Vosges	56. Loire	86. Pyrénées Orientales
28. Haut Rhin	57. Rhône	87. Bouches de Rhône
29. Loire Atlantique	58. Ain	88. Var
	59. Haute Savoie	89. Corse

stabilisation;

(5) completed crisis: severe drop in economic and demographic rates (Dordogne, Aveyron, Indre).

Figure 5.3 is a theoretical model which does not imply an inevitable development. The beginning of the cycle and the rhythm of its movements can both be very variable.

Subdued and completed crises are by their very definition old crises, for the most part initiated as long ago as the nineteenth century, and by now having reached a very advanced stage. The new feature is the dive towards completed crisis, a veritable liquidation of the region. Active crises are more recent; they are at the start of the cycle. The special case of the active industrial crises of the North-East frontier is attributable to the present regime and, in particular, to the European Coal and Steel Community. It should be emphasised that these situations are the most serious.

It should also be noted that the rhythm of development of crises is faster during the present period and that at the same time subduing occurs much more quickly. Finally, it can be established that under the guise of spatial and regional policy the monopolies and the State carry out a policy of relieving active crises by locating industries employing

Figure 5.2: Categories of Crisis in France

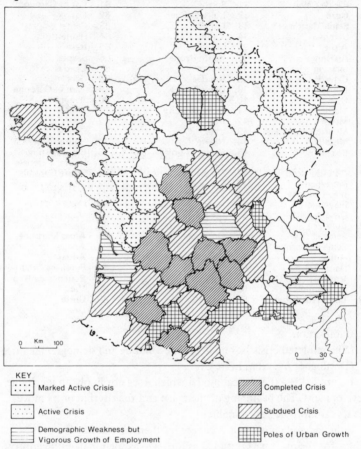

KEY

:::: Marked Active Crisis   Completed Crisis

...... Active Crisis   Subdued Crisis

        Demographic Weakness but   Poles of Urban Growth
        Vigorous Growth of Employment

Figure 5.3: The Crisis Cycle

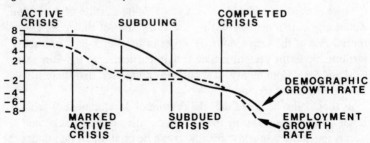

Annual rates of growth (in relation to the age group entering
the labour market)

unskilled and underpaid labour in areas with a relative labour surplus.

The 'Regulation' of Regional Crises

It is in the nature of regional crises that they can be compensated for and instantaneously regulated. Such regulation was easier to perform when capitalism was in a boom period and needed large quantities of labour.

'Regulation' by Migration

To fill the 3.9 million jobs available (maintained and created) between 1962 and 1968, the system had 'at its disposal' 3.5 million young people entering the market and brought in 650,000 active immigrants – leaving a not inconsiderable margin of unemployment. It should be emphasised that at the same time the number of French workers crossing the North-Eastern and Eastern Frontiers was increasing: nearly 30,000 new frontier workers crossed to Germany and Switzerland.

Active Foreign Immigrants. Active immigrants of foreign origin are preponderantly male (three-quarters are men) and adult (one-third are young people). It can be noted that during this period foreigners had already been used to cushion violent shocks to the labour market. In Lorraine, the number of foreigners at work fell by nearly 12,000, making it possible to 'limit the damage'. If this reduction and the increase of frontier workers is taken into account, the result in Lorraine would be a shortage of male jobs of more than 50,000 (not 33,700 as appears at first sight). The mechanism of reversal to which those in power have resorted for two years had already been developed by the steel industry.

While immigrants from abroad – primarily foreigners – may have played the chief part in the adjustment of the capitalist labour market, internal migration should not be discounted, particularly since it provides an excellent insight into regional situations. The following analysis refers to the internal migration of active male workers.

Internal Migration. The migration of young people (15-31 years) should be distinguished from that of other age groups, allowing the following cases to be identified:[1]

(1) Regions with low rates of migration: Picardie, Haute-Normandie, Champagne, Ardennes, Franche-Comté. There is an exodus of young people, but this is very moderate (about 2.5 per cent).

(2) Nord and Lorraine have high rates for young people and still higher rates for adults. Industrial crises, in this phase, have brought about a higher rate of departure for adults than for young people.
(3) The West has highly contrasted migratory movements, with a high rate of departure of young people (between 15 and 20 per cent in general) and a much lower rate of adult immigration. The balance is strongly negative. Bourgogne is a separate case with quite large movements in both directions (departures of young people — adult arrivals). Limousin has even more violent movements.
(4) The regions of Aquitaine, Midi-Pyrénées, Languedoc-Roussillon and Centre have a fairly substantial departure of young people (5 to 10 per cent) but a very much larger adult immigration (10 to 20 per cent). Two cases can be distinguished: Languedoc and Centre with a very great expansion of employment on a moderate demographic base; Aquitaine and Midi Pyrénées with a moderate growth of employment and a very poor demographic situation.
(5) Apart from these, there remain important special cases: Alsace appears to be an 'exceptional' case, with young people arriving and active adults leaving. In fact, the Alsatian labour market at this time had a very special trend, since the regional balance of employment was practically nil while the flow of manpower towards Germany and Switzerland was developing vigorously. Rhône-Alpes attracts both young people and adults, the total of internal migrants representing 10 per cent of young people from the region entering the labour market. Provence-Côte d'Azur is the most 'attractive' region in France, with an equal entry of young people and adults, representing nearly 30 per cent of the region's young age group.
(6) There remains finally the very special case of the Paris region. The internal migratory balance is relatively modest, about 10 per cent, but this is the result of considerable movements in opposite directions: young people arriving (+ 30 per cent); adults leaving (– 20 per cent).

The Paris region obviously plays a national role. It is the 'throbbing heart' of France, involving all the regions (only Provence, Rhône-Alpes and Alsace have a migratory system relatively independent of Paris). The Paris region attracts young manpower and drives out adults. The monopolies and the State have developed a system of exploitation specific to the region, which is revealed by the 'consumption' of younger labour more suited to the form of over-exploitation represented by work and life played to the tune of Paris. It can also be noted that the

age structure of foreign immigrants is likewise very different between
Paris and the provinces, amounting in essence to the provinces receiving

Table 5.2: Migration of Active Young People, 1962-68

Departure		Arrival		
Rate 〉per cent		Paris region		108,000
West	77,500	Provence)	17,000	
Rate between 5 and 8 per cent		Rhône-Alpes)	13,000	30,000
South West, Massif Central,		Alsace		3,600
Centre, Bourgogne, Nord,				
Lorraine	54,000			
Rate around 2 per cent				
Picardie, Haute-Normandie,				
Champagne, Franche-Comté	8,500			

Table 5.3: Migration of Active Adults, 1962-68

Departure		Arrival		
Paris region	72,500	Provence, Côte d'Azur)		33,000
Nord, Lorraine	25,000	Languedoc-Roussillon)		
		Aquitaine)		25,000
Paris Basin (Haute and)		Midi-Pyrénées)		
Basse-Normandie, Picardie,)	2,800	Centre		13,000
Champagne))		Other regions:		
Franche-Comté-Alsace)		Rhône-Alpes, Massif)		
		Central, Bourgogne,)		30,000
		West)		

adults and the Paris region young people. The Paris region is
undoubtedly the essential element in the migration of young people,
receiving more than three-quarters of the flow, whilst with adult movements the case is different.

Adult movements are essentially away from the Paris region and the
areas of active industrial crisis and towards the demographically weak
areas of Southern France, the Mediterranean and the South-West.

Taken together, the two great 'rivers' of migration are the movement
of young people away from active crisis areas towards the Paris region
and the movement of adults away from the Paris region and industrial
crisis areas towards the demographic crisis areas of the South (the Mediterranean region and the area of absorbed crisis of the South-West and
Centre).

There is no doubt, therefore, that there is 'compensation' between
the different types of regional crisis. What sets France apart is that this

compensation is not made directly but rather through the mediation of the Paris region.

'Regulation' through Unemployment

We have measured unemployment as a rate of 'numbers becoming unemployed', equal to the percentage of those becoming unemployed during the period in question in relation to the regional demand for employment (entry of young people from the region on to the labour market adjusted by the migration balance of active young people). While the national average (for men) is 5.5 per cent, regional rates vary widely: from 1.1 per cent in the Pays de la Loire to 14.1 per cent in Provence-Côte d'Azur. The levels of unemployment are remarkably structured, closely linked to regional migratory balances. The rates of numbers becoming unemployed are practically nil in regions with a nil migratory balance and they rise regularly in line with the migratory balance, whatever the direction of this balance may be.

To put it another way, there are two types of unemployment, different in range and significance. There is *unemployment of departure*, widespread in the West and especially in Nord and Lorraine, therefore involving regions in active crisis and exerting the pressure which triggers off migratory movements, that is departures. It is a pressure previously brought to bear on young people. There is also a systematic *unemployment of arrival*, varying in severity with the extent of the migratory balance. This type of unemployment has another significance: according to a well known mechanism, it is bound to ease pressure on wages in areas which have a large number of job vacancies. In these areas it is in the monopolies' interest to have a fairly high level of unemployment in order to maintain the 'fluidity' of the labour market and, especially, to counteract any tendency for a rise in wage levels.

Under these conditions, it is normal for the Paris region to stand out, with a rate of people becoming unemployed of 7 per cent, while the provincial maxima (Lorraine on the one hand and Centre on the other) are about 5 per cent. There are two exceptions – Nord and Provence. In these regions a very pronounced 'excess unemployment' has been demonstrated: 8.75 per cent in Nord and 14.1 per cent in Provence-Côte d'Azur. In Nord it is a question of excess unemployment of departure linked with a certain resistance to leaving, particularly among young people. In a region with no tradition of migration the crisis on the labour market has had an intensity which has taken people by surprise and the migratory reflex seems to have been triggered off rather late. The Census of 1975 shows that things have since settled down and that the young people of the Nord have also begun to leave.

As far as Provence-Côte d'Azur is concerned, there is an enormous excess unemployment of arrival linked to very special conditions of regional employment: a high proportion of foreign workers and the important role of construction (and tourism) in the economy.In a region where economic development has had a markedly speculative character it has been to the advantage of the system to have available a pool of unemployed labour to avoid an escalation of wages. There is a certain anarchy in regional employment but it is a deliberate anarchy which acts in the interests of a speculative economy.

The New Impetus Given to Regional Crises by the Establishment of State Monopoly Capitalism

State Monopoly Capitalism inherited a series of regional crises which had been under way for a long time in some cases; it has created new regional crises by plunging previously prosperous areas into active crisis. The influences associated with State Monopoly Capitalism are of two types: the aggravation of absorbed crisis with the slide towards accomplished crisis, revealed by the virtual despoliation of several parts of the country; and the amelioration of active crises, particularly in agriculture, for the sake of locating labour-intensive industries. The new crises created by the system are the industrial and mining crises of Nord-Pas-de-Calais and Lorraine, directly connected with European integration, with the abandonment of national mineral resources.

However, all these crises took place during the period 1962-8 against an overall background of capitalist boom which had two sets of consequences at the regional level. The first was the existence of areas of accelerated growth: the Paris region, the Mediterranean, the Lyons area. These areas of growth have extremely serious problems: shortage of facilities, all kinds of difficulties for workers, speculation of all kinds, etc., but they are none the less employment poles attracting both internal and external migrants. Second, by means of a process of 'crisis − migration − unemployment', an attempt is made to regulate regional crises on a national scale. Unemployment forces moves which relieve crises. This process is centred on the Paris region, which is not only by far the foremost French region but also the regulating centre of all regional crises in France. In other words, during a boom period, capitalism has quite easily retained 'mastery' of regional crises and can even pride itself on some success in that field.

The equilibrium obtained is the result of an adjustment between four factors. First, the development of active crises and a relative surplus of young workers. Second, the intensification of absorbed crises and the existence of a labour shortage over a large part of the country. Third, the development of a unique 'system of exploitation' in the Paris region, which is actually a system of super-exploitation based on the labour of young people, which sets in motion a migratory pump fed by the surpluses and shortages existing in the provinces. Fourth, the presence of large numbers of immigrant workers, who have to stand the shocks of growth and contraction alike. During a boom period a kind of equilibrium can be achieved which is in effect only an adjustment of imbalance.

So, the State boasts of having 'balanced' migration in the Paris region with that of the rest of France. In terms of the overall balance of jobs this is apparently true but the real flows are intensifying and reflect three crisis situations:

the employment crisis of the West and Nord;
the demographic crisis of the South;
the crisis of modes of life and work in the Paris region.

Regional Change since 1968: the Build-up of Crisis in the 'System of Regulation'

What has become of the regional crises and the system of regulation with the development of the general crisis since 1967-8? With more limited figures than those used for the analysis of the earlier period, we can put forward tentative conclusions.

The active population in work increased by 1.1 million between 1968 and 1975, at a pace quite comparable with that established previously. However, the regional spread of this growth has become modified: there has been a marked slackening in the Mediterranean and Atlantic regions — this group of regions only absorbed 27 per cent of the additional active workers, compared with 40 per cent between 1962 and 1968. On the other hand, the acceleration of growth is noticeable in the Paris Basin and, especially, in the East. The decline in the predominantly rural regions can be understood in the light of the intensified agricultural crisis (the active agricultural population fell by 3.6 per cent per year between 1962 and 1968; the fall was 5 per cent after that) but this does not explain everything. Other factors must also be taken into account. These will be shown in the analysis of the development of the active wage-earning population (that is in sectors other than agriculture) and unemployment.

The Development of Paid Employment since 1968

On average, this has grown at a very slightly higher rate than during the period 1962-8. But this does not mean that nothing new is occurring, rather the opposite. Two phases should be distinguished: from 1968 to 1971 and from 1971 to 1974, the year of greatest growth before the recession.

The first developments of the general crisis of the system appeared in the course of the early years. But they were not yet so noticeable as to appear in the regional pattern, especially since these years were characterised by a strong economic situation, following the victories of the popular movement of May-June 1968. The structural weaknesses of certain regions were even temporarily hidden (cf. the sharp expansion in the South-West, Auvergne and Bourgogne). But the general situation remained the same: pursuit of strong growth to the west of the Paris region; pursuit of stagnation in Nord and Lorraine; strong growth of the capital region. However, new situations were taking shape: high growth in the frontier areas of the east (Alsace and Franche-Comté), fairly appreciable reduction in the Mediterranean region.

In the course of the second period, after 1971, elements of prime importance appeared. In the provinces the growth of employment continued at the same pace (2.3 per cent per year) but the slowing down on the national scale arose from a reversal of the situation in the Paris region: the employment growth rate fell by half (1.15 per cent per year); in volume the region absorbed 14 per cent of the extra jobs, instead of 25 per cent as before. In the provinces, the behaviour of the different regions tended to return to that prevailing before 1968 but with more marked divergences (greater growth in the Paris Basin and the West, slowing down in the South-West, more and more pronounced stagnation in Nord and Lorraine). However, certain trends which had been developing since 1968 became established: vigorous growth in the East, especially Alsace, and an accentuation of the slow-down in the Mediterranean South.

The Development of Unemployment

Up to 1974, total unemployment remained steady (753,000 in 1971 and 757,000 in 1974) but in slightly modified form: a reduction in the Paris region, the Paris Basin and also in the Eastern Central area, an increase in the South and the South-West and also in the East, in spite of the development of employment. There is therefore no similarity between the map of unemployment and the map of employment; the chief feature is the position of the capital region, where the very slight number of jobs created does not bring about the development of unemployment.

From 1974 to 1975, unemployment 'blossomed', reaching 1,151,000 in March 1975. The increase was high in all regions, the lowest rate of increase being 18 per cent in Auvergne. But it was felt especially in France north of the Loire, reaching a peak in Alsace (167 per cent). Let us emphasise the position of the Nord region ('moderate' increase), the Paris region and Rhône-Alpes (the only ones approaching the national average).

The rise in unemployment has continued since 1975. In one year unsatisfied demand for employment increased on a national scale by 35 per cent; the geographical distribution was more even but, all the same, the East's record (56 per cent) must be stressed.

The Development of Crisis in the 'System of Regulation'

What significance can be given to the trends that have been outlined? The deepening of the general crisis of State Monopoly Capitalism did not reveal itself mechanistically in the same way in all regions: because their structures are different and because they are not watertight compartments separate from each other. The period between 1971-2 and 1976 was one of transition: tendencies established during the growth phase and new tendencies coexisted, but the latter were only beginning.

Thus, the long-standing deep crisis of Nord and Lorraine worsened; but even so it can be said that the rise in unemployment there was relatively modest. The novelty, therefore, lay in the development of emigration. In the West and the greater part of the Paris Basin the agricultural crisis levelled out, while the number of 'decentralised' jobs created increased (this ceased two years ago (in 1974) but the integration of the regions into a new system of regulation has not yet occurred). For long-standing crisis areas like the South-West and the Massif Central, there was a tendency to reproduce the previous situation but at an even lower level.

On the other hand, the first developments of the general crisis immediately caused difficulties in certain regions. The management of the crisis by drastic cuts in the national budget halted the speculative euphoria which was taking the place of growth on the Mediterranean front; to some extent it was a mechanical effect. In the Paris region the recession had deeper roots and still more serious effects, since it had immediate implications elsewhere, given the central position of the capital in the general system of regulation.

Gradually a new trend appeared: *the displacement or spreading of the crisis of the Paris region to other regions with no possibility that this would resolve the severe problems of the capital*; the average increase in unemployment together with the recession in employment reflected the modification of migratory movements with the provinces. A similar phenomenon occurred in the frontier regions, which 'picked up' the crisis from neighbouring countries: there the expansion of employment was, and now that of unemployment is, largely due to the trans-frontier structure of the labour market.

Can it be said that we are heading towards a new system of regulation? Doubtless, but it is still too early to be sure. Up to now we have experienced only the first phase of the regime's crisis. The most serious regional effects are still to come, when the Seventh Plan is put into action. Thus a region like Rhône-Alpes, which seems to be more strongly resistant than others, will be rapidly confronted with the monopolies' international restructuring.

One thing is certain: the new regulation can only be a crisis regulation, with limited effectiveness. Economically, this system cannot avail itself of the relative 'rationality' which characterised the previous one; 500,000 unemployed can be managed by inter-regional modulation, this can no longer be done with 1.5 million unemployed. The social and political consequences are obvious and the State tries to concentrate action on this plane, in particular by avoiding excessively high levels of unemployment whenever this could most rapidly lead towards questioning of its domination. The main orientation is therefore towards the greatest possible distribution of unemployment and the assumption of responsibility for it by levels other than the centre.

The Monopolies – the State – the Regions

A crisis makes problems strangely complicated and the management of a crisis of this extent is no small task. Presidential tricks are soon used up. In regional affairs something new must be found.

The first requirement, from the monopolies' point of view, is mobility of capital and labour. Crisis involves permanent redeployment, a feverish search for a loophole in the market and for a reserve of labour at the cheapest rate. This takes place against a background of permanent instability and uncertainty, since production and markets are subject to restructuring and international agreements which can instantly turn their operating conditions upside down. Monopolies must be able to make very rapid changes in production methods, location and labour. They therefore need great fluidity in the labour market, a new mobility in the population and a development of migration.

The main problem for the State is to provide more massive finance for French-based monopolies, feeding monopoly accumulation with public funds. This implies elsewhere a policy of austerity, cutbacks and economy in public services. In effect the State has adopted a policy of austerity and new economies. Thus it is that the Seventh Plan tries to make savings on the cost of urban growth by putting a draconian brake on the expansion of big conurbations, beginning with the Paris region. This implies a reduction of inter-regional migratory balances. During a crisis phase, then, it is a question of achieving a simultaneous development of migratory movements and a reduction of overall movement. This is quite possible provided there is a very precise and very effective means of regulating migratory movements.

Finally, there is the search for a new means of 'regulating' migration. The system of crisis — migration — unemployment worked well enough for capitalism during the boom period. It no longer works today. The increase and generalisation of unemployment have made it obsolete as a means of regulating migration. All the regions today are permeated by structural unemployment, of both departure and arrival. In addition, for obvious political reasons, the State has to check this unemployment to avoid dangerous pockets and, therefore, has to conceal its regulatory character to an even greater extent.

Under these conditions the problem can only be solved by very delicate State intervention at all levels and in all areas: teaching and vocational training; employment agencies; disturbance allowances for young people, etc. This is certainly the direction the State is taking. Great efforts are being made and a structure is being set up for the control and precise management of the labour market and of occupational and geographical mobility. But all this intervention is aimed at managing the French population as far as possible to suit the needs of the monopolies, while these same monopolies are constantly changing course in response to alterations in economic circumstances.

The management of a crisis is an attempt to bring order to fundamental chaos, and attempts to resolve certain contradictions only make matters worse. The truth is, no solution is possible under the present system without a means of imposing mobility on people to suit the requirements of the monopolies. But as it happens, people are less and less inclined to comply. Here too the system is reaching its limits . . .

This is shown in the political sphere by a double movement. On the one hand, the global crisis seems to overlay and standardise regional crises. Everyone is similarly affected by unemployment and austerity.

But at the same time and precisely because there is a global crisis, the system tends to lose control of regional crises. Serious cracks have already appeared; others are on the way.

Appendix: Methodology and Definitions

Almost the only source used is the Institut National de la Statistique et des Etude Economiques (INSEE) Census, or more exactly, the two censuses of 1962 and 1968. For the period after 1968 there are the employment surveys and the evaluation of the active wage-earning population made by INSEE. The basis of this work is a comparative study of two censuses, in order to find the answer to a precise question: what is the position, in each region, of the new generation entering the labour market? The entry of young people into this market seemed to be the best indicator of the regional situation, particularly since that indicator is itself of considerable interest.

To answer this question we have developed a new method which we will call the 'sliding census' method, which consists of comparing the results of the two censuses for each age group and each region. Without wishing to enter into methodological detail here, let us say simply that comparison of the age structure of active workers between one census and the other makes it possible to form a precise idea of development during the period, by showing: the number of young people of a particular region starting work in the region; the number of young people from outside a region starting work in the region; the number of young people leaving a region; and the number becoming unemployed. It is also possible to compare the arrival of young people on the labour market (entries) with the withdrawal of old people through retirement or death (departures); equally, one can compare demographic flow with economic movement: jobs created and jobs lost.

This last point represents the principal element of our analysis. It gives us, in effect, an interesting picture of the regional situation since the demographic flow (entries and departures from the market) gives an idea of the demand for jobs in the region, while economic movement (jobs created and jobs lost) makes it possible to appreciate the degree to which this demand is satisfied, at least on a quantitative level. On a subsidiary level, the method offers the advantage of measuring regional migratory movements by the balance of natural changes which gives much more reliable results than the figures provided by INSEE on this. Briefly, it can be said that censuses tend seriously to underestimate migratory movements: the margin of error is already very wide in the 1968 census (it is incidentally likely to be much greater in the 1975 census).

Vocabulary and Concepts Employed

Demographic Flow. Entry of young people of a region on to the labour market (between 15 and 31 years for men, between 15 and 28 years for women); cessation of work by adults and old people: the sum of deaths of active people and retirements from work.

Migratory Movements. The balance of migration of active workers (internal and external) is calculated, on one hand, for young people, on the other for adults and old people. If the migratory balance of young people is positive, it is added to the entry of young people of the region, to give the 'employment demand' in the region (conversely with a negative migratory balance). If the migratory balance of active adults is positive, it reduces by the same amount the jobs left, to give the number of jobs made available (the converse applies with a negative migratory balance).

The Movement of Employment. During the period there has been a development of employment itself, with jobs created and jobs lost. We have evaluated it by major branches, by totalling the positive and negative balances appearing under the heading of jobs created and jobs lost (there is a simplification in so far as it is in fact a question of balances in major branches). For jobs created we have separated the roles of government and the economy. By convention, we have considered jobs lost as essentially affecting the adult and aged section of the population. To put it another way, we have subtracted the number of jobs lost from the number of jobs made available (cessation of work − migratory balance) to obtain the number of jobs maintained and available for young people. Here there is an element of convention which does not affect the calculation since it involves comparing different flows. The jobs available finally put on to the labour market are the sum of jobs maintained and jobs created during the period. The regional employment demand is finally divided between those starting work (equal to jobs available) and those becoming unemployed.

Note

1. Migratory movements have been calculated as a percentage of the young age-group entering the labour market. Thus, for example, for Basse-Normandie: arrival of young males on the labour market: 68,600; balance of internal migrations of active young workers: − 11,150; rate of migration of young people: − 16 per cent.

6 REMARKS ON THE SPATIAL STRUCTURE OF CAPITALIST DEVELOPMENT: THE CASE OF THE NETHERLANDS

Dieter Läpple and Pieter van Hoogstraten

Introduction

The process of development of the economies of the highly advanced capitalist countries has resulted, within recent decades and especially within the last two crisis cycles, in an accentuation of the uneven distribution of social production within space.

The dichotomy created during the Industrial Revolution between industrialised agglomerations and non-developed rural regions has become more intense. Nowadays, in addition, important differences between industrialised regions have been created; in particular, there are severe disproportions within the spatial structures of the advanced urban agglomerations. In the analysis of highly advanced capitalist countries, these processes of development confront us with the problem of the simultaneous coexistence of both development and underdevelopment. The integration of the problem of uneven spatial development in the analysis of highly advanced capitalist countries becomes more urgent as these forms of uneven development are made an issue in the class struggle. The confrontations between the various classes and strata in society over the creation and use of socio-economic areas increase in number and in intensity, as one can easily see in various countries.

Until recently in theoretical discussions, this problem was almost exclusively dealt with on the level of the international market. On this level it was elaborated and analysed in terms of the coexistence of chronic underdevelopment in Third World countries and expansion in highly advanced industrial states. In the analysis of the uneven spatial development within the highly advanced capitalist countries it was obvious to refer to contributions to an explanation of uneven or underdevelopment as they had been worked out in the analysis of peripheral capitalism. Some reference to these theories of uneven or underdevelopment is also prompted by the fact that the 'centre-periphery relation' can be quite clearly traced in the superficial appearances of the processes of uneven spatial development within the developed capitalist countries. In this way one can point to the accentuating polarity between urban growth centres and underdeveloped peripheral regions.

Even in some of the most important theoretical contributions towards the explanation of uneven spatial development within highly advanced capitalist countries, elements from explanations as they have been put forward in the analysis of peripheral capitalism can be easily detected.[1] This applies above all to the theory of the *transfer of value* and to the *'dependencia' discussion.*[2] The former explains underdevelopment by the thesis of a continuous transfer of value created in the periphery to the centre. The main representatives of this interpretation are Amin, Emmanuel, Palloix and Mandel. The explanations evolved within the Latin American 'dependencia' discussion are mainly based on the thesis of the structural heterogeneity of social production; the uneven and combined development of capitalist, semi-capitalist and pre-capitalist relations of production lies at the base of uneven development.[3]

In our opinion it is problematic to adopt these kinds of contributions in explaining the uneven development of the social process of reproduction within industrialised countries.[4] It is beyond the scope of this chapter to give a detailed critique of these kinds of methodological approaches but the reasons why we see them as problematic can be spelt out.

First, in so far as these contributions to the explanation of underdevelopment are not directly derived from modification of the law of value — i.e. derived from the limitations and possible modifications which result from the national state being the political organisation of capital — underdevelopment is derived from particular features of the historically specific form of development and the functioning of the general laws of accumulation of capital within the heterogeneous relations of production in the periphery. It is obvious that the processes of uneven development of socio-economic structures *within* highly advanced capitalist countries cannot be explained from the modification of the law of value on the world market — a proposition which is, in our opinion, insufficient in any case.[5] Uneven development can neither be explained directly from existing heterogeneity (if any) within the relations of production nor from the heterogeneity in levels of productivity in different sectors of production. The existence of semi- or pre-capitalist relations of production (e.g. handicrafts, parts of agricultural production) and of barely developed branches (e.g. parts of medium and small business) can reinforce the unevenness of the processes of development but it cannot be the motive for the latter's existence. Indeed, in our analysis the starting-point is the thesis that the *processes of uneven spatial development* are actually being aggravated by the *tendency of the homogenisation of production*. This tendency towards the homogenisation of production is the result of the continuing integration of production into the world market. It comes about especially by way of the destruction of that part of production which was previously intended for the regional market. The integration of production into the world market occurs through the development of multinational concerns, while smaller national or regional capitals either become integrated or vanish in cut-throat competition.

The formation of supranational entities such as the EEC means intensified reorganisation – for a large number of branches of production because the tariff and monetary barriers between the member states are being removed. It was precisely these branches of production – at least in the Netherlands – that, in the past, lessened the unevenness of spatial development because of their relatively decentralised spatial structure. This point will be elaborated later.

Second, the spatial dimension has not been systematically integrated in theories of underdevelopment. These theories contain an implicit reference to space, but the question of the spatial differentiation of the social process of reproduction as an essential part of uneven development has not been adequately explored. The spatial dimension is expressed either merely in the boundaries of the organisation of capital within a national state, or, in rare cases, by further elaboration on the urban-rural dichotomy. This dichotomy is viewed not so much as an aspect of spatial structure but rather as an expression of heterogeneous relations of production. In addition, it has to be stressed that the question of uneven development in advanced capitalist countries cannot be reduced to the simple polarity of urban centres and underdeveloped peripheries. The development of society leads to highly differentiated spatial structures in the social process of reproduction. In this process not only are severe disparities and marked economic dependence created between regions but also this process entails a strong spatial segregation of social functions within different regions: The social process of development occurs in this way in ever more complicated and interdependent spatial structures which are determined by the increased uneven development of social reproduction.

In this chapter we want to set out in the form of a number of hypotheses how a materialist explanation of the processes of uneven spatial development can be elaborated. Before doing so we want to emphasise that the question of spatial structure cannot be reduced to 'infrastructure' or 'built environment' in the sense of 'spatial preconditions' for socio-economic processes as has been assumed in several theories. Since the spatial dimension forms a constituent moment in the social process of development, spatial structure also has to be analysed as the immanent result of social development. As will be obvious by now, in our view the explanation of the processes of uneven development has a crucial function in this.

First of all, we will attempt to give an explanation of both aspects of the problem — spatial or territorial structure and uneven development — in their relation to one another based on the laws of the development and functioning of capitalist reproduction. In the following three parts of this chapter an analysis will be made of the degree to which these spatial structures and tendencies, as they result from the internal laws of capitalist development, can be traced in historically concrete regional development in the Netherlands. In the first of these an explanation will be given of the historical determinants of the socio-economic and spatial structure of the Netherlands. The next part contains comments on the methods which are necessary to relate the empirical statistical data and the — abstractly formulated — laws of development to each other. Then the empirical data will be presented and interpreted. The different steps in the analysis of uneven spatial development in highly developed capitalist societies as presented in this article are only first attempts. In further research these steps must be elaborated into more highly differentiated ones and be related to each other more closely.[6]

Theoretical Outlines

Spatial Structure — Result of Relations of Production

The starting point in our analysis is that the spatial structure of the social process of reproduction, as well as the processes of development and restructuring which occur in this structure, have to be analysed as the *result* of the historically specific form of production existing at a certain time. In our case this means: as the result of capitalist relations of production.

It is vital that in an analysis of uneven spatial development one first of all gets an insight into the tendencies of uneven development and spatial division as they result from the *immanent laws* of capitalist production. The overall spatial division of population and social production — and in particular the uneven character of this division — is heavily dependent on the particular historical process of the disintegration of the feudal mode of production and the allied development of capitalist relations of production. Only after formulating the immanent laws is it possible to indicate how these specific capitalist tendencies of development, in combination with the simultaneous disintegration of the former relations of production, have advanced and revolutionised the social process of reproduction according to their logic. It also has to be pointed out how the capitalist process of accumulation in its turn creates the conditions for its own negation. In addition, of special interest in the analysis of the spatial structure of the social process of reproduction is *the way in which* the spatial structures encountered in the historical process have been transformed by the dynamics of the development of capitalist accumulation — whether they have simply been undermined and replaced by new, different structures, or whether these encountered structures, for example pre-capitalist cities, have been dissolved in the motion of capitalist accumulation and reproduced at a higher stage as results of their own logic of development.[7]

On the Problem of Uneven Development

As we will point out more fully further on, the extent and concrete appearances of uneven spatial structures are in their nature essentially determined by the historical stage of development of the capitalist mode of production.

The fundamental *cause* of unevenness reproducing itself more intensely, however, must be sought in the immanent tendencies of capitalist accumulation. In the capitalist process of accumulation as a process of continuous expansion of surplus-value production and as a process of incorporation of the surplus value appropriated by the capitalist into the continuously increasing amount of capital, the capitalist mode of production itself produces the pre-conditions for its continuity and expansion. In particular, it produces the maintenance and expansion of the division of classes into wage labour and capital.

In this process of maintenance and expansion, capital is forced by competition to overcome the limitations and constraints occurring in this process by *increasing the productivity of social labour*. Such an increase of productivity, however, is only possible for capital by increasing the *scale of production* which is itself dependent on the rate of *expansion of individual capitals* based on capitalist property relations. The decisive forms of growth of individual capitals as *preconditions* for the capitalist form of the development of the productivity of social labour are the concentration and centralisation of capital in terms of value. By the movement towards concentration of capital we mean the process of growth of individual capitals by the transformation of produced and appropriated surplus value into capital. In this movement, the expansion of capitals takes place as an *uneven process of growth* on account of differences in initial sizes, in which the bigger capitals, as a rule, have a head start because they are able to organise their labour process on a higher level due to their bigger mass of capital. By doing so, they are able to make a much more intensive use of the general causes of the growth of productivity of labour such as co-operation, division of labour, etc. The tendency towards the transition to the growth form of centralisation is embedded in the uneven process of growth of individual capitals. In the centralisation of capital the growth of individual capitals does not simply come about by the conversion of surplus value into capital, since the limitations to growth resulting from the constrained mass of surplus value for appropriation are also overcome by the absorption of hitherto independent capitals: the expropriation of capitalists by capitalists.

This movement of centralisation is by no means a one-way process. Besides the centralisation of capital, there will always be the creation of new individual capitals. Centralisation, as the growth form of capital, leads, despite the ever-operating tendency towards the equalisation of rates of profit, to an 'internal differentiation in the structure of capital as a whole into big centralised capitals'.[8] This *systematic differentiation in the structure* of the process of growth of capital as a whole which results from the overall tendencies of accumulation of capital lies at the heart of the processes of uneven development in the capitalist mode of production.

However, to be able to explain the relation of interconnection between the tendency present in the process of accumulation of capital to an uneven development of total social capital and the creation of uneven spatial structures of the social process of reproduction, we will need an intermediate link. In our argument until now, we have limited ourselves to the value aspect; i.e. we have concentrated on the growth in value of individual capitals as a *pre-condition* and as a *result* of the development of productivity under capitalist relations of production. The actual development of productivity, however, is carried into effect through the concrete *material* side of the process of production: through the labour process. Thus, to be able to explain the forms in which the tendency towards uneven development of total social capital come about, we will have to analyse the social process of production in its *contradictory unity of being a process of labour and a process of surplus-value production*. With this line of approach, it will be possible to analyse the interconnection between the tendency towards uneven development (in terms of value) of total social capital and the creation of uneven spatial structures in the social process of reproduction. The dual character of the process of production gives us the decisive methodological starting-point for the systematic integration of the spatial dimension into the analysis of the social structures and processes of development.

On the Problem of Integrating the Spatial Dimension into the Analysis of Social Processes

Although every kind of social labour necessarily contains a spatial aspect, the integration of the spatial dimension into the analysis of social processes has not yet been satisfactorily achieved.[9]

In our opinion, the decisive methodological approach for the integration of the spatial dimension lies in the recognition of the dual character of social labour. From this viewpoint, social labour can be analysed both as a process of metabolic interaction between man and nature (i.e. the aspect of the determination of human labour and human life in general by nature) and at the same time as a process of the specific socialisation of human life (i.e. the aspect of the determination of the form of social labour by the particular relations of property and production).

For a society based on the production of commodities, this means that each of the sectors of production, which have developed within the framework of the social division of labour, are determined by nature each in its own way and to different degrees. In such a way a *spatial division of labour* develops alongside the social division of labour.[10] The dependence of the different material processes of production on the given natural conditions in space is nevertheless not unchangeable. These conditions, due to their characteristic of being limitations to production 'lying outside the production process itself'[11], are steadily forced back with the development of social potentialities — as will be elaborated later. Hence the territorial division of labour is less and less determined and fixed by immediate given natural conditions. In this process of developing the productivity of social labour, the social conditions of production, i.e. the economic, social and politically mediated conditions of production and reproduction, become ever more important. To clarify what particular spatial structure is produced by the capitalist mode of production and how the former develops in connection with the uneven accumulation of capital, we will have to look at the development of the spatial division of labour in relation to the specifically capitalist form of the development of the productive forces.

Spatial Structure in the Process of Development of the Capitalist Mode of Production

The development of spatial structure in the capitalist mode of production comes about on the historical basis of the *division between town and country*. However, this does not imply that the tendencies of spatial development, which are immanent in the capitalist mode of production, can be explained by this urban-rural opposition. The existence and functioning of these tendencies already presume the historical development of this dichotomy. The fundamental result of the historical development of the urban-rural opposition is the dispossession of the direct producers of their means of production and subsistence resulting from the replacement and dissolution of feudal relations of production in the countryside: thus, the creation of the 'free' wage labourer. This is the pre-condition in terms of class structure for the full development of industrial production.

A spatial division of labour, which has developed progressively, occurs in connection with the industrial division of labour based on this class structure; i.e. on account of the laws of the capitalist mode of production, a specific spatial structure develops. Hence spatial structure is determined by the growth and spatial movements of capital, by which individual capitals are drawn to those places where they can find the best opportunities for their processes of surplus-value production because of the *natural and social conditions* for their specific processes of production existing at those places. This spontaneous and socially unplanned process is regulated by the immanent law of movement of the capitalist mode of production — the law of value which makes its influence especially felt socially in the form of cyclical crises. In this way the spatial division and restructuring of social production occurs through the results of the processes of crisis which arise in the accumulation of capital.

In this process of the spatial differentiation of social production, which proceeds under the imperatives of permanent competition, the choice of location for individual capitalists in the early stages of capitalist development was still very dependent on the 'natural' conditions of location (e.g. the availability of raw materials, natural routes of transport like navigable rivers). This direct dependence of production on factors of location determined by nature, however, is in contradiction with the tendency of capital to emancipate itself from all limitations to surplus-value production 'lying outside this process itself'. Accordingly, the capitalist mode of production has, in connection with the development of the productive forces, increasingly disengaged itself from its original basis, nature. The conditions of production have been shifted from immediate natural conditions to general interlocking relationships within production, the creation of which is mediated by exchange value. This, however, does not imply that in consequence the dependence of social labour on nature has been abolished. On the contrary, along with the growing potentialities of *social* production, the dependence of production on the natural basis also increases — only this dependence takes the shape of an ever more mediated form. In this way the development of bulk transport through pipelines gives the opportunity to build oil refineries on almost any site in the world but the construction of a system of pipelines simultaneously limits more strongly than ever the choice of location of an oil refinery. Thus, development of the productive forces makes capitalist production even more independent of the limitations which are imposed by the 'natural' conditions of location. At the same time, however, the spatial division of the social process of reproduction is progressively more subjected to the conditions of valorisation of capital by the capitalist form of the development and use of the productive forces. Development of the productive forces in particular branches such as the petrochemicals industry can imply complete restructuring of those areas where those branches of production were located previously or where those branches are going to locate.[12]

Apart from the general tendency that capitalist production is continually emancipating itself from the immediately available 'natural' conditions of production and hence is increasing its potential spatial mobility, what are the remaining tendencies in spatial development that can be deduced from the specific capitalist form of the development of the productive forces? To give an answer to this question we will now have to investigate the effects on spatial structure of the processes of concentration and centralisation of capital in terms of value and the tendencies embedded in these processes towards the uneven development of capitalist production. In doing this we will have to limit ourselves to some of the main theoretical points because we are dealing here with an interconnection between many processes, some of which are also mutually contradictory.

The concentration and centralisation of capital in terms of value are, as we have seen, pre-conditions for the increase of productivity of social labour. However, the development of the productive forces can only come about by way of the concrete material processes of labour. This occurs when the potentialities which result from co-operation and the division of labour[13] are further developed by systematic organisation and changes in production and when, at the same time, the potentialities of free natural forces[14] are integrated into the process of production on a higher level. As this is only possible by the spatial concentration of labour power and means of production, the development of production leads thus to a *spatial concentration of the productive forces.*

Labour power and means of production, however, are not both subjected to this process of spatial concentration in the same way. From a certain stage in the development of the mode of production the volume of means of production increases faster than the amount of labour power. This can be deduced from the fact that from a certain stage in the development of the productive forces, their development is directed above all at raising the level of surplus-value production through the saving of human labour ('the economy of living labour'). This process can even lead to a situation where, along with a rise in the level of production, an 'absolute' expulsion of labour power occurs and this leads to a reduction of the amount of agglomerated labour power.[15] However, this tendency towards spatial concentration and centralisation of the productive forces as it results from the development of the productivity of labour says little about the tendencies of spatial polarisation resulting from it — which are above all based on the 'internal structural differentiations' of the process of growth of total capital resulting from accumulation at the level of individual capitals. It also says little about the specific spatial structure of the capitalist mode of production.

The spatial structure of the social process of reproduction cannot be understood from the analysis of the development of productive forces in the immediate process of production of capital alone. For this we will have to concentrate especially on the interconnection between the individual elements of the social process of reproduction. The social mechanism of production and reproduction has been broken into splinters by the social division of labour and these parts have become formally independent of each other. Hence, the understanding of spatial structure as the result of the social division of labour presupposes an understanding of the internal interconnection and the totality of the social process of reproduction. The concept of the 'social collective labourer'[16] gives us the analytical entrée. With this notion the structure and development of the socialisation of labour in its dual character (as concrete useful labour determined by nature on the one hand and as abstract labour whose form is socially determined on the other) can be captured conceptually. The social collective labourer does not only include the labour functions within immediate material production. It includes all productive and unproductive functions in total social labour, which have become an interconnected system in the social division of labour through the process of capitalist development. As the development of productivity is always directly related to the expansion of the division of labour, both within each individual firm and at the level of society, it leads to an increasing differentiation of the social collective labourer. The social division of labour which determines the structure of the social collective labourer is partly the result of the separation of labour functions within the interconnected system of the already existing processes of production and partly the result of the creation of new labour functions.

As we have already indicated, from the social division of labour (by branches or functions) a spatial division of labour also develops. Thus, by way of this process of differentiation by the division of labour of the social collective labourer, the development and the restructuring of spatial structure come about. The relationship between the division of labour by branches or functions and the spatial division of labour can be established by means of the twofold character of labour. The location, or integration into the spatial structure, of the partial functions that have become 'independent' in the process of the further differentiation of the division of labour is determined by their mutually different dependencies on spatially given, *naturally determined productivity* and on *socially determined productivity* which is connected with the different locations. The former refers to the *natural* conditions of production (the availability of raw materials, climatic conditions, etc.) and the latter to the *social* conditions of production (the existing stage of socialisation of production, level of qualification of the labour force available in the region, the reserve of labour, wage level, etc.). The determination of the locations of these 'partial functions' of the social collective labourer, however, does not result from the particular demands of their separate labour processes. From the process of the *division* of labour originates the necessity to *interlock* social labour, i.e. the systematic arrangement of these formally independent partial functions, within the complex totality of interdependent relations where partial functions and totality are both pre-conditions of each other. The development of the productivity of labour is not only dependent on the further development of the division of labour by branches and functions of production, as it also results from the planned restructuring and rationalisation of the immediate process of production of the individual capitals. Along with the increasing socialisation of production, the productivity of social labour becomes ever more strongly dependent on the possibilities of the systematic combination in space of the different stages of production. Besides this, it also becomes increasingly more dependent on the economic and social functions coupled with but outside material production; for example, the functions of circulation or aspects of the reproduction of the labour force. On the one hand, the social division of labour develops and deepens as a result of integration into the world market and the aggravating pressures of competition. On the other, the social connections of labour — i.e. the systematic combination and co-ordination of the partial functions of the social process of reproduction which have become formally independent in the development of labour — are established on the basis of the mechanism of price and profit.

In this way the contradiction on the level of the socialisation of production, which is embedded in these complementary processes, is exacerbated. In other words, the division of labour between branches and functions — which is forced regardless of the social organisation of the process of reproduction — reaches an ever greater contradiction with the needs for territorial and functional interconnections, or spatial socialisation. On account of this internally contradictory process of development and the resulting economic and social conflicts, economic and political structures develop which have the purpose of creating possibilities for movement and development *within* private capitalist conditions of production in order to increase the level of socialisation of production.[17]

For the partial realisation of these interlocked and interconnected relations, which become ever more necessary, 'chains of production',[18] organised on a private capitalist basis, develop — mainly through the monopolistic structures of production — which are the result of the systematic differentiation of the process of growth of capital. Spatially they are reflected in regional or *'territorial complexes of production'*. Such spatial complexes of production, with their increasing mutual differentiation, can also lead to territorial or spatial specialisation between the complexes themselves. They can originate in the combined use of the specific conditions of location in an area (e.g. the so-called 'sea port complexes'). They can also originate from the combined sequential linking of stages in the production of particular products or systems of products on the grounds of a common basis of production (e.g. the petrochemicals complexes).

Along with the formation of these complexes of production, it also becomes necessary to develop complementary branches of production and services — for example, the production of the general conditions of production and of reproduction of the labour force. These all-embracing complexes of production and functions are no longer created exclusively — at least if they are to function adequately — by way of the spontaneously and anarchistically functioning mechanism of price and profit. Primarily, this is closely bound up with the high degree of socialisation that is necessary for the creation of those complexes. In consequence, direct intervention of the state becomes necessary.

The spatial structure, however, is not only based on the immediate material functions of social collective labour; it is also influenced by the so-called 'tertiary functions'. Because of the complexity and the heterogeneity of these tertiary functions, we can only mention some of them. Our main concern here is to elucidate the interconnection with material production. A fundamental part of the tertiary functions, especially the functions related to the increasing scientisation of production (research and development etc.), services and maintenance, but also different commercial, administrative and juridical functions, could develop into independent parts of the social collective labourer only after a certain stage in the development and concentration of material production had been reached. These functions were initially organised as secondary functions of the collective labourer — at the level of the firm — within the framework of industrial production. The marked spatial concentration of industrial production offers the possibility of centralising these functions, which are dispersed among different firms, in independent firms and by this organisation on a higher level, to perform these functions more effectively and economically. In the tertiary functions of transport, or in the sphere of circulation of commodities, the same interconnections with the locations of industrial production exist. Once such tertiary functions have developed into independent spheres, the relationship in which they are directly determined by existing industrial production slowly dissolves and changes into a relationship which is characterised by interaction. Within this relationship these functions can develop their own patterns of location. This means that the very spatial concentration of such tertiary functions in its turn becomes a pre-condition for the existence and further development of industrial production in a particular spatial context. What we have outlined here for the 'production-orientated' tertiary functions applies also to the tertiary functions which are orientated to the reproduction of the labour force. The provision of the latter functions by private capitals, but also to an increasing extent by the state, is dependent (or is made dependent) on the existing density of population, in order that the optimal economic use can be made of them.

In the examination of the differentiation of the social collective labourer by the division of labour, we have concentrated until now on the processes which are related to a tendency towards spatial concentration and centralisation of the productive forces. We will now pay attention to the question of possible *tendencies of decentralisation*.[19] In the process of the differentiation of the social collective labourer partial functions which have completely different requirements of location from the functions of production to which the former were previously related in one homogeneous process of production, are unlocked. In this way, through this differentiation, the *possibility* has been created of organising these specific functions of production as an independent firm in a new optimal location. In this process of separating one or more partial functions, however, the problem of establishing and maintaining the functional interconnection with the forward and backward stages of production and also with the necessary non-material labour functions must have been solved. This implies that such processes, as a rule, can only take place in the form of *subsidiaries* within the framework of the structures of big enterprises. By means of these subsidiaries, usually limited to one phase of production, labour-intensive functions of production, for example, can be transferred to areas with a large reserve of labour and with a low wage level. As the question of subsidiaries has been treated at greater length in other places we will not pay any more attention to it here.[20]

Beyond these possible processes of decentralisation which result from the spatially selective differentiation of the social collective labourer, there are also tendencies of decentralisation which are the immediate results of the processes of concentration and centralisation. Such tendencies of decentralisation are more or less immediate results of the processes of expulsion which originate in large part from competition for industrial and commercial areas which are principally limited in areas of agglomeration and for the relatively scarce labour force. From these processes of competition for the spatially limited or scarce conditions of production, so-called 'filtering down' comes about; i.e. the selective expulsion of economically weak firms or entire branches of production. The actualisation of these tendencies of decentralisation is highly dependent on the course of the crisis cycle — e.g. the decentralisation processes resulting from competition for spatially limited conditions of production occurs almost exclusively in periods of economic expansion.

Without treating the problems related to the tendencies of centralisation at great length here, we are still able to formulate the hypothesis that in the operation of the tendencies of spatial concentration and centralisation it is not at all a matter of equivalent and mutually equalising tendencies. From the laws of development of the capitalist process of reproduction, a clear dominance of the tendencies towards spatial concentration and centralisation becomes evident. As we have argued above, the tendencies of spatial development, as they result from the internal laws of the capitalist process of development, unfold starting from the *already available historically determined spatial structure*. As the most salient phenomenon, one has to point to the fact that those spatial structures, at least overall, are reproduced with an astonishing continuity. In this process of reproduction of disparate spatial structures, with the increasing development of the capitalist mode of production the spatial agglomeration of the productive forces (including the conforming structures of urbanisation, conditions of reproduction of the labour force, etc.) has become steadily more and more the pre-condition for the further development of the productive forces. The social process of development presupposes ever more 'prior conditions' (for example, specific interlocked relations between production functions and labour functions, a minimum level of the agglomeration of the labour force possessing specific skills, the availability of the general conditions of production and the general conditions of the reproduction of the labour force) which can no longer be taken care of by individual capitals. To an increasing extent the situation is created whereby the development of capital and revenues for the capitalist class can only develop when their pre-conditions are made available from public resources. This 'parasitic' process of development of capital not only leads to a permanent reproduction and aggravation of underdevelopment in 'rural areas' but also, along with the expanded reproduction of urban agglomerations, to a disintegration of spatial-social interconnections.

To conclude this section, it has to be noted that the tendencies of spatial development in the current stage of capitalist development are aggravated principally by the strengthening of tendencies of over-accumulation, the falling tendency of the rate of profit and by the actions and strategies of capital and the state to counteract these. The theoretical structure which we have outlined is the framework necessary for the interpretation of the concrete historically occurring processes of development in particular regions. However, we immediately have to make the qualification that in this chapter it is impossible systematically to mediate the tendencies of spatial development as they result from the general laws of capitalist development and concrete historical appearances. Such a procedure presupposes a systematic analysis of the historical course of the process of capital accumulation, of the complex class confrontations and class struggles and of the specific intervention by the state in the process of social reproduction. We will have to limit ourselves to a rough outline of the inter-regional division of labour and uneven and inter-regional development using different structural indicators. Before this inter-regional analysis of the structure of economic development in the Netherlands, a brief review will be given of how the processes of regional development in the Netherlands are currently dealt with.

Comments on the Current Discussion of Dutch Regional Structure

'The West' and the 'Rest of the Netherlands'

Traditionally, one talks about regional development in the Netherlands in terms of a bipolarity. On the one side there is 'The West' ('Het Westen'), which is roughly formed by the provinces of Noord-Holland, Zuid-Holland and Utrecht, and on the other hand the 'Rest of the Netherlands' ('Overig Nederland').[21] 'The West', the 'Randstad' or the 'Ring-city' is, in this conception, the geographical expression of the agglomeration of capital and labour; the 'driving-force of our national economy'.[22] The 'Rest of the Netherlands' is almost hanging off, as the term itself suggests. Here dispersed activities of secondary importance take place.

Recently, more differentiated approaches to this situation have been proposed. Lambooy and Huizinga draw attention to the creation of an 'accretion area' which has been formed by the 'swelling' of the Randstad'.[23] The 'Old' West together with this accretion area constitutes the 'New West'. This accretion area is an intermediate zone, which differs from the Old West but because of the strong concentration of social activities there, it has to be added to the latter. The Randstad swells into a second ring and the rest remains paralysed by its 'economic and social inertia'.[24] Empirical data on the development of population, shares of gross regional product, level of income and the sectoral division of economic activities – all very aggregate statistics – are used to prove the existence of the accretion area. They observe that the 'dominance of the West of the country' has indeed become weaker and that the adjoining belt has been strengthened, but that there has remained a clear partition: the (New) West and the 'Rest of the Netherlands'.[25]

Without any clear theoretical framework, evidence is trotted out for a phenomenon already known from the practice of regional policy, namely that the traditional boundaries of the Randstad are no longer

Figure 6.1: The 'New West' in the Netherlands

KEY

a. Veluwe
b. Veluwe Fringe
c. Rest of Zeeland; Walcheren-Zuid Zeeland
d. Western part of Noord Brabant
e. Nieuwe Waterweg

f. Zwolle
g. Arnhem-Nijmegen
h. Ijsselmeer polders
i. Mijnstreek
j. Zaanstreek

used for an effective policy. Their motive for the analysis is thus more to criticise the policies than to contribute to an understanding of the relationship between national and regional development. The intermediate zone is only understood as an expansion of the Randstad. However, with such an approach the differential character of the processes which lie at the basis of the 'swelling' of the Randstad cannot be grasped. The empirical data for the new division into areas (figures on the development of the population, regional shares in the Gross National Product (GNP), the regional division of employment and income) are draped around the bipolarity without any explicit theoretical concepts. For an understanding of the character of the 'swelling' of the Randstad, it is vital to elaborate the great variety of processes of development underlying it. The accretion area consists of different zones, each of them possessing very different spatial structures, which have to be understood from the specific historical starting-point and the dynamics of the change of regional structure:

(1) In the Veluwe (see Figure 6.1) changes in the regional structure are mainly determined by the suburbanisation of the Randstad with its related problems of commuting, infrastructure, welfare amenities and environment and by the fact that the Veluwe-fringe is on a continuation of the axis of development of the service sector in the west of the country, in which Utrecht absorbs an important part of the growth.

(2) The incorporation of the accretion area 'Rest of Zeeland' into the New West is solely caused by the integration of the island of Walcheren/Zuid-Beveland into the petrochemicals complex of Rijnmond (the mouth of the Rhine) and the Schelde Basin. Here a special form of industrialisation has taken place, where a completely new industrial structure, consisting exclusively of monopolistic petrochemical, biochemicals and metallurgical firms, has been imposed on the former ways of life.

(3) The incorporation of the western part of Noord-Brabant into the New West has a great variety of causes:

    (i) suburbanisation; this zone functions as a residential area for the Nieuwe Waterweg area in particular;

    (ii) because of the existence of nuclei of development, new activities in both manufacturing and service sectors have developed or existing firms have been able to prolong their life. Partly this relates to subsidiaries of multinational enterprises and to processes of 'filtering down', i.e. under the pressure of a tight labour market a 'weak' firm, for example, disappears from the Randstad to 'peripheral' regions:

(iii) on account of its situation on an axis of development the region also has its own tendencies of development, such as the growth of the service sector, which cannot be directly explained by radiation from the Randstad.

(4) In both Zwolle and the Arnhem-Nijmegen area different processes are operative. Most importantly, these areas have a very stagnant economic structure.

Figure 6.2: Dutch Regions

A second contribution to give a more differentiated approach to the traditional view on regional structure is that of the Centraal Plan Bureau (Central Planning Office).[26] As in the first contribution, the expansion of the Randstad is the central starting-point. The 'radiation of activities' is thought to be related to distance from the metropolitan centres in the Randstad. In this way three areas are distinguished (see Figure 6.2). First of all, there is the Noord-Holland and Zuid-Holland area which is characterised by a strong concentration of economic activities and population. The second area consists of the neighbouring provinces of Zeeland, Noord-Brabant, Utrecht and Gelderland. These provinces have common features in that they are situated a short distance from the metropolitan centres and that the dispersion of activities and population from those centres is directed to them. The third area is formed by the outer fringe of the provinces of Friesland, Groningen, Drente, Overijssel and Limburg. Because of the great distance, the radiation of activities will be weaker and this will express itself especially during periods of economic stagnation.[27]

In more detail than the first contribution, a *description* is given of the developments in the socio-economic structure of the individual provinces — using structural *and* cyclical indicators. The model of explanation based on the expansion of the Randstad is relativised. 'Growth impulses, for example, will not come from the area indicated as the centre but also from others.'[28] However, structural changes in the individual regions are not analysed in their mutual interconnection, while the framework in which an explanation of these developments can be looked for is also lacking. Structural changes in the Dutch economy, which can be understood from its internal contradictions and related integration into the world market, produce different effects in the different regions. Therefore developments in the regions can only be analysed in their mutual relation of interdependence.

Opening Remarks on the Empirical Analysis of Dutch Regional Structure

Historical Determinants

As we have shown above, the internal laws of development of capitalist production determine the development of each individual region. The concrete course and form of regional development, however, is also the result of the specific way in which the historically and spatially given structure forms the framework for the functioning of the laws of development. In our empirical analysis we will concentrate only on the most important post-war changes in regional structure. The historically evolved structures which create the material base for the processes of restructuring and the international context, which determines these processes to a great extent, can only be dealt with briefly.

Many authors recognise strong continuity in the development of Dutch spatial structure; clearly historical determinants fulfil an important role in spatial development. Jansen and de Smidt's formulation is that 'the vitality of the old centres of production', despite the deterioration of the locational factors available there, 'should not be underestimated.'[29] A clear example of this is the Mijnstreek (the mining area) in the southern part of the province of Limburg, a region which since the closure of the collieries has had anything but radiant 'vitality'. In former times a carbo-chemicals complex had developed there on the basis of the on-the-spot extraction of coal. Along with the replacement of the raw materials base — from coal to oil and natural gas — made possible by technological development and made necessary by economic development, a new chemicals complex has been created within the existing regional structure, although the previously decisive locational factor — the availability of coal — had disappeared. So, spatial structure is known to have an important historical component.

The foundations of the actual regional spatial structure were laid during the Industrial Revolution, which in the Netherlands only came very late compared with the other Western European countries and so had a very uneven and *spatially dispersed character*. This was closely bound up with the structure of Dutch capital which in those days had found its goal in foreign investment and in trade. It paid hardly any attention to the development of national industry. The absence of iron ore and the unfavourable location of the coalfields did not permit, in the first instance, the development of a heavy metals industry, 'the steaming and straining heart of industrialisation'.[30]

Besides the industrial centres in Rotterdam, Amsterdam and the Zaanstreek (Zaan region) which were based on the processing of colonial products and were suited for this by their maritime situation, industrial centres also developed in eastern Groningen, Twente and the eastern part of Noord-Brabant and in the south of Limburg. They were situated far from one another, had little or no relationship with each other and in almost none of the places were wage labourers more than 20 per cent of the working population. Each of the regions mentioned

here had, by its specific structure, the character of its soil and the composition of its population, particular natural and social conditions for
the emergence of certain forms of regional development. For the
centres in the West this has already been touched on. For Twente,
eastern Groningen and the eastern part of Noord-Brabant, besides the
widespread availability of cheap labour because of the historical socio-
economic structure, the industrial structure mainly developed on the
basis of *agricultural production.* [31] For southern Limburg, the specific
geographical, financial, economic, political and technological factors
formed the basis of the — late — exploitation of the coalfields without
leading to the formation of an integrated coal, steel and chemicals complex, as occurred in the Ruhr. [32]

The International Framework

The socio-economic and spatial structure developed in this way is being
replaced and changed by processes of internationalisation. This internationalisation has to be looked upon both from the aspect of *integration into the world market* and from the aspect of the *destruction of
traditional, regional-market-orientated manufacturing*. It is exactly this
context in which regional development has to be analysed.

Within the Western European countries in general, and within the
EEC in particular, there is the question of a strong intra-industrial
division of labour. This can be deduced from the intensity and the
growing intensification of intra-community trade. This process has been
accelerated by the formation of the EEC and the related removal of
barriers to trade, but before this happened the process was already
clearly present. [33] The main determinant of the development of the
spatial structure of Western Europe is the increasing concentration of
industrial production in the core of an area which is formed by an
industrial axis running from mid-Italy to the Netherlands, interrupted
only by the Alps. Across the sea this axis of development is extended
through England. This implies that approximately two-thirds of social
activities take place on about one-third of the land surface. Within this
industrial belt we can distinguish areas of concentration in the triangle
Lille-Randstad-Ruhr, southwards in the Rhine-Mainz area and the
Rhine-Neckar area and over the Alps in the northern Italian industrial
triangle Genoa-Milan-Turin. Apart from this tendency towards reinforced concentration of industrial production in the areas mentioned
here, there are two other fundamental movements in spatial development. They are the *'westward orientation' of flows of commodities*
and the *transfer of industrial activities into the coastal regions.* Both

tendencies are mainly due to the reinforced dependence of European industry on overseas raw materials and an increasing export orientation.

Returning to socio-economic structure, we can say that the Netherlands had a low degree of industrial development at the beginning of the 1950s compared with most other Western European countries. The principal characteristics of Dutch industrial structure were: (a) the processing and finishing of agricultural products and (b) manufacturing based largely on unskilled or semi-skilled labour. Both categories accounted for a much higher share of industrial production than in most other Western European countries. In addition the Dutch economy, in particular in the West of the country, was strongly orientated towards trading functions. In subsequent years the growth of employment in industry lagged behind that of other EEC countries, while at the same time the structure of industrial production shifted more strongly than elsewhere towards capital-intensive branches, in which skilled and highly skilled labour was increasingly required. The development of the tertiary sector occurred more markedly in the Netherlands than elsewhere. In summary, these structural changes in the Dutch economy occurring in an international framework affect regional development in different, uneven and selective ways.[34]

Method and Statistical Data

The concrete economic structure of a region and its development are the results of a complex process of socio-economic development causing particular forms of inter-regional division of labour. These particular forms are strongly historically determined. The changes in the economic structure of the Netherlands, occurring more rapidly and strongly since the 1960s, involve strong spatial shifts. This applies for the major nuclei in both production and consumption.

The processes of restructuring which occur in different regions, have distinctive causes:

economic-technological changes, especially changes in the production process;
changes in the energy and raw material base of production;
changes in the system of transport and communication;
creation of new sectors of the economy;
changes in the structure of the world market because of the shift in flows of commodities and changes of the division of labour on a global scale.[35]

Additionally, political changes, like the creation of supranational political structures such as the EEC, also play an important role. Within the process of regional development and restructuring, many of these causes are interwoven. Of critical importance, however, are economic-technological changes.[36] All these processes are related to changes in class and exploitation relations. The course of these processes of restructuring is always interconnected with and essentially determined by confrontations between classes and class fractions. Within this framework the central economic and political function of monopoly capital must be emphasised. Important contributions to the analysis of this problem are made by Damette (see Chapter 4).

An approach involving various levels has been proposed by Claussen and Läpple[37] which allows us to gain an insight into the evolution of spatial structure in relation to different socio-economic processes of development within the 'systematic differentiation in the structure of capital' — the basis for the processes of uneven regional development. Briefly, these levels can be summarised in the following concepts: *analysis of structure, analysis of interlocking relations* and *analysis of development.* The *analysis of structure* is mainly concerned with the (formal) reproduction of the internal articulation of a regional economic ensemble. In an *analysis of interlocking relations*, the forms of interdependencies between the various parts of the structure, particular forms of socialisation of production, have to be analysed. Through the *analysis of development*, the causes of the processes of development and change are clarified and indications of possible future directions can be formulated.

In the following sections we will deal with aspects of the analysis of Dutch regional economic structure. An articulation of a complex and interdependent regional economic ensemble will be given from two viewpoints in the form of an inter-regional comparison of economic structure. One perspective is a division into economic groups (Tables 6.2 and 6.3) and the other is a division of industry and manufacturing into different types of commodities in order to show the existing structure of branches of production (Tables 6.6 and 6.7). In the context of the consequences of territorial socialisation for regional development, the analysis of interlocking relations is of special importance. In such an analysis, the relations should be investigated from three closely connected aspects, which together form a contradictory unity: from the value aspect; from the aspect of the material form and from the aspect of property relations. However, such an analysis of interlocking relations cannot be elaborated in the context of this article. As we will limit our analysis to a survey of inter-regional relationships, aspects of the analysis of interlocking relations and development will be dealt with only in so far as this is necessary for the interpretation of changes in regional economic structure.

To conclude this part, some remarks are made on the statistical data used in the following analysis. The official statistics available for the analysis of regional development only partially[38] reflect the complex processes of regional change. A brief discussion of the data we have used underlines this. We will start with the most exact data: the censuses of population. Starting with the viewpoint that changes in material production determine the structural changes in regions, despite their precision these censuses give an inadequate picture of the dynamic development of regional structure. The development of the size and composition of the population in a region is the result of numerous different processes, like the growth or decline of employment, suburbanisation, a declining fertility rate, etc. Development is likely to be the outcome of these concurrently occurring processes. The figures on population say hardly anything about regional structure.

Paradoxically, the data which reveal more about the actual development of regional structure are also more unreliable since they are inadequate estimates. Although the development of Gross Regional Product (GRP) and the size of the labour force give a more adequate picture of the development of regional structure, they too are the outcome of many contradictory processes. An increase in the gross product of a region (irrespective of the way the GRP is made up) can indicate, for example, a quantitative extension of existing production or, alternatively, an increase in labour productivity. In the latter case a large increase in the GRP can even coincide with a substantial reduction in the labour force in the region. An increase in the number of jobs in certain border provinces, for example, could be an indication of a strengthening or a weakening of the industrial structure – despite the 'moderate optimism' of some policy-makers about their policy of decentralisation. A weakening can occur when firms, and even entire branches, which cannot manage any longer in competition for labour power and space in the Randstad, move to the 'peripheral' provinces ('filtering down'). Of all the statistical data under review here, the development of investment in fixed assets gives the best reflection of changes in regional structure, but they are also the most unreliable. An additional difficulty which occurs here is that these data only reflect *movement*; they do not give an insight into the *determining factor* of the spatial structure: the development of fixed capital in its quantitative and qualitative dimensions.

Main Developments in Dutch Regional Structure

Empirical Framework

The empirical framework for our analysis is given in Tables 6.1 to 6.3. Table 6.1 gives the division of the industrial employed population and the population by provinces and major regions. The relatively stable character of the structure can be readily observed in the changes in the proportions of population of the provinces and major regions. This stability cannot be interpreted as static but rather as the reproduction of historical structures. On this basis social developments take place which change these historical structures. The relation between total population and employed population in the Northern provinces in 1930 was the reverse of that in the West. Over the years the difference between the proportions of population and employed population has diminished in the 'rural' provinces, while in the West it has increased.

The differences in the relation between population and employed population in the Northern agricultural and the Western provinces in 1930 and the further development of this relationship in the North indicate the shrinking role of agriculture in the economic structure. Allied to this was the dissolution of the family as the unit of labour which in turn formed the basis of the integration of women into the process of industrial production. In 1930 this process was already in full swing. The same applies to Noord-Brabant and the East where a great part of this high proportion of women in industry is because the men's wages are inadequate for bringing up a family. Especially in 1975, the difference between population and employed population in the West has become bigger, which points to the process of suburbanisation taking place mainly in the direction of Noord-Brabant and Gelderland. So we see that shifts in the division of the population, though small, involve different, hidden processes. The impact of these shifts on the structure of employment will be elaborated later.

Table 6.2 gives an inter-provincial comparison of the proportions of industrial sectors in GNP for the years 1960, 1965 and 1970. It gives an indication of the 'productive power' of each province. Together with Table 6.3, which gives the intra-provincial division of the shares of sectors in GRP, this enables us to give an overall assessment of the mutual and interdependent shifts in provincial economic structures. The last column of Table 6.2 shows that the net effect of the shifts between 1960 and 1970 has only been small. Nevertheless, there has

Table 6.1: The Distribution of Total Population and Employed Population in the Netherlands by Provinces and Major Regions, 1930-75

	1930		1950		1963		1975	
	Total Popn.	Employed Popn.	Total Popn.	Employed Popn.	Total Popn.	Employed Popn.	Total Popn.	Employed Popn.
Groningen	4.95	4.54	4.54	4.15	4.09	4.04	3.94	3.78
Friesland	5.04	3.12	4.60	3.03	4.10	3.25	4.07	2.61
Drente	2.80	1.43	2.81	1.69	2.73	2.07	2.95	1.93
NORTH	12.79	9.09	11.95	8.87	10.92	9.36	10.96	8.32
Overijssel[a]	6.56	9.31	6.71	9.00	7.05	7.05	7.19	6.47
Gelderland	10.45	10.89	10.83	10.87	11.27	9.90	11.92	10.94
EAST	17.01	20.20	17.54	19.87	18.32	16.95	19.11	17.41
Utrecht	5.13	5.14	5.75	5.82	5.96	5.58	6.31	6.81
N-Holland	19.02	19.36	18.44	18.84	17.86	19.79	16.80	18.82
Z-Holland	24.67	24.56	23.85	23.40	23.44	25.49	22.24	24.44
WEST	48.82	49.06	48.04	48.06	47.26	50.86	45.35	50.07
Zeeland	3.12	2.22	2.67	2.19	2.40	2.05	2.40	2.09
N-Brabant	11.32	14.63	12.47	15.00	13.25	13.12	14.27	13.81
Limburg	6.94	4.81	7.33	6.01	7.81	7.65	7.68	6.89
SOUTH	21.38	21.66	22.47	23.20	23.46	22.82	24.35	22.79
TOTAL	100	100	100	100	100	100	100	100

Note: [a] Overijssel includes Ijsselmeerpolders.
Sources: W. Steigenga; TESG, 1958; CBS Bedrijfstelling 1963 deel 3 regionale ulkomsten; CBS, Bevolking der Germenten 1-1-63 en 1-1-79; Statistick Wreksame Personen 75.

Table 6.2: Percentage Shares of Provinces and Regions in GNP by Sector, 1960-70

	Agriculture, Fishing and Forestry			Mining, Manufacturing Construction and Utilities			Transport and Communications			Others (Trade, Banking, etc.)			Industry (Columns 1-4)			Public Sector			Total (Columns 5 and 6)		
	60	65	70	60	65	70	60	65	70	60	65	70	60	65	70	60	65	70	60	65	70
Groningen	6.24	4.68	5.70	3.80	3.94	4.64	4.66	3.62	3.26	3.76	3.54	3.61	4.10	3.84	4.18	3.71	3.83	3.73	4.06	3.84	4.13
Friesland	7.71	7.48	8.21	2.84	3.07	2.51	2.80	2.74	2.32	3.21	3.20	3.04	3.45	3.45	3.10	3.27	3.20	3.26	3.43	3.42	3.12
Drente	9.09	4.25	5.67	2.12	2.08	2.21	1.77	2.04	1.30	1.73	1.76	2.16	2.23	2.15	2.36	2.36	2.36	2.42	2.24	2.17	2.36
NORTH	23.04	16.41	19.58	8.76	9.09	9.36	9.23	8.40	6.88	8.70	8.50	8.81	9.78	9.44	9.64	9.34	9.39	9.41	9.73	9.43	9.61
Overijssel	9.09	9.16	10.64	7.09	7.21	7.08	3.98	4.27	3.95	5.15	5.28	5.58	6.44	6.48	6.46	5.58	5.93	6.12	6.35	6.42	6.42
Gelderland	12.82	12.63	13.56	9.41	9.93	9.98	6.94	8.52	7.29	9.03	9.07	10.28	9.45	9.74	10.13	12.53	12.00	13.41	9.76	10.01	10.59
EAST	21.91	21.79	24.20	16.50	17.14	17.06	10.92	12.79	11.24	14.18	14.35	15.86	15.89	16.22	16.59	18.11	17.93	19.53	16.11	16.43	17.01
Utrecht	4.05	4.35	3.96	4.73	4.93	4.36	5.06	4.62	4.61	6.12	6.28	7.07	5.13	5.35	5.64	8.09	7.59	7.39	5.43	5.61	5.86
N-Holland	12.48	12.59	11.53	18.71	17.52	17.21	22.35	22.00	20.09	25.50	25.07	21.85	20.56	20.06	19.02	17.86	18.59	18.45	20.29	19.28	18.95
Z-Holland	20.42	22.84	16.68	24.85	24.55	25.82	38.72	37.32	43.51	28.54	28.44	26.80	26.63	26.27	26.72	25.89	26.33	24.31	26.56	26.67	26.42
WEST	36.95	39.75	32.17	48.29	47.05	47.57	66.13	63.94	68.21	60.16	59.79	55.72	52.32	51.68	51.33	51.84	52.51	50.15	52.28	52.16	51.23
Zeeland	6.47	5.18	5.19	1.74	1.90	2.74	1.93	1.72	1.70	2.02	1.97	2.11	2.32	2.19	2.59	2.24	2.20	2.25	2.32	2.19	2.53
N-Brabant	10.62	11.53	13.24	15.60	16.04	16.08	6.49	8.01	7.04	9.34	9.84	11.06	12.39	12.92	13.13	12.75	12.51	12.84	12.43	12.84	13.09
Limburg	5.54	5.33	5.58	9.11	8.78	7.37	5.30	5.19	4.95	5.51	5.55	6.47	7.29	7.11	6.67	5.68	5.73	5.83	7.13	6.95	6.56
SOUTH	22.63	22.03	24.01	26.45	26.72	26.19	13.72	14.92	13.69	16.87	17.36	19.64	22.00	22.22	22.39	20.67	20.44	20.92	21.88	21.98	22.18

Sources: CBS Regionale Rekeningen 1960 en 1965; CBS Regionale Economische Indikatoren 1970.

Table 6.3: Shares of Industrial Sectors in GRP by Provinces, 1960-70

NORTH

	Groningen 1960	Groningen 1965	Groningen 1970	Friesland 1960	Friesland 1965	Friesland 1970	Drente 1960	Drente 1965	Drente 1970	NORTH 1960	NORTH 1965	NORTH 1970
Agriculture, fishing, forestry	14.83	8.94	8.18	20.58	16.01	15.59	19.05	14.32	14.20	17.58	12.74	12.07
Mining, manufacturing, construction, utilities	42.23	44.90	43.85	49.84	39.15	31.41	42.76	41.90	36.53	40.63	42.13	38.01
Transport & communication	7.82	6.28	5.41	5.54	5.32	5.09	5.38	6.24	3.76	6.95	5.92	4.90
Other industries	26.05	28.08	31.34	14.60	28.45	34.91	22.34	24.69	32.78	25.87	27.44	32.85
Industry (rows 1-4)	90.93	88.19	88.78	90.56	88.94	87.00	89.54	87.15	87.27	90.48	88.24	87.83
Public sector	9.07	11.81	11.22	9.44	11.06	13.00	10.46	12.85	12.73	9.52	11.76	12.17
Total	100	100	100	100	100	100	100	100	100	100	100	100

EAST

	Overijssel 1960	Overijssel 1965	Overijssel 1970	Gelderland 1960	Gelderland 1965	Gelderland 1970	EAST 1960	EAST 1965	EAST 1970
Agriculture, fishing, forestry	13.10	10.45	9.81	12.03	9.25	7.62	12.46	9.72	8.45
Mining, manufacturing, construction, utilities	50.41	49.19	43.02	43.51	43.36	36.93	46.23	45.62	39.23
Transport & communication	4.27	4.43	4.22	4.84	5.60	4.74	4.62	5.14	4.54
Other industries	23.47	25.05	31.13	26.78	27.59	34.94	25.47	26.60	33.49
Industry (rows 1-4)	91.25	89.07	88.17	87.16	85.81	84.23	88.78	87.08	85.70
Public sector	8.75	10.93	11.83	12.84	14.19	15.80	11.22	12.98	14.30
Total	100	100	100	100	100	100	100	100	100

WEST

	Utrecht 1960	Utrecht 1965	Utrecht 1970	N-Holland 1960	N-Holland 1965	N-Holland 1970	Z-Holland 1960	Z-Holland 1965	Z-Holland 1970	WEST 1960	WEST 1965	WEST 1970
Agriculture, fishing, forestry	6.83	5.67	4.00	5.63	4.64	3.62	7.04	6.28	3.74	6.47	5.59	3.72
Mining, manufacturing, construction, utilities	39.37	38.78	29.03	41.62	38.53	35.41	42.24	40.25	38.11	41.70	39.43	36.07
Transport & communication	6.34	5.48	8.08	7.50	7.36	7.65	9.92	9.32	10.41	8.61	8.16	9.12
Other industries	32.67	33.99	43.21	36.53	38.40	41.23	31.13	32.47	36.32	33.38	34.90	38.93
Industry (rows 1-4)	85.20	83.99	84.32	91.27	88.93	87.91	90.33	88.31	88.58	90.16	88.09	87.84
Public sector	14.80	16.01	15.68	8.73	11.07	12.09	9.66	11.69	11.42	9.84	11.91	12.16
Total	100	100	100	100	100	100	100	100	100	100	100	100

SOUTH

	Zeeland 1960	Zeeland 1965	Zeeland 1970	N-Brabant 1960	N-Brabant 1965	N-Brabant 1970	Limburg 1960	Limburg 1965	Limburg 1970	SOUTH 1960	SOUTH 1965	SOUTH 1970
Agriculture, fishing, forestry	25.60	17.34	12.03	7.82	6.58	5.98	6.99	5.62	5.04	9.43	7.35	6.40
Mining, manufacturing, construction, utilities	33.89	38.05	41.89	56.68	54.62	47.91	57.67	55.26	43.82	54.59	53.18	46.01
Transport & communication	5.67	5.21	5.47	3.55	4.16	3.68	5.06	5.03	4.82	4.27	4.53	4.22
Other industries	25.30	27.47	29.67	21.76	23.35	30.25	22.37	24.33	35.30	22.33	24.07	31.68
Industry (rows 1-4)	90.46	88.07	89.06	89.81	88.70	87.83	92.09	90.24	88.97	90.62	89.13	88.31
Public sector	9.54	11.97	10.94	10.19	11.30	12.17	7.91	9.76	11.03	9.38	10.67	11.69
Total	100	100	100	100	100	100	100	100	100	100	100	100

NETHERLANDS

	1960	1965	1970
Agriculture, fishing, forestry	9.16	7.33	5.91
Mining, manufacturing, construction, utilities	45.15	43.72	39.00
Transport & communication	6.18	6.66	6.85
Other industries	28.96	30.45	35.87
Industry (rows 1-4)	90.08	88.16	87.58
Public sector	9.92	11.84	12.42
Total	100	100	100

been a relative decline in the position of the West. As with Table 6.1, the stability expressed in this table is the result of the reproduction of the historically developed structures.

The first problem which arises with such an outline is in classification and stems from the heterogeneity of the different forms of regional development. Yet in a memorandum of the Committee of the European Community in 1969, it was concluded that the following tripartite division was meaningful for a classification of regions:

(1) industrialised regions, characterised by highly developed industry, less than 10 per cent agriculture, a high population density, well developed infrastructure and a well developed tertiary sector;

(2) semi-industrialised regions, characterised by initial industrialisation, a barely significant tertiary sector, a relatively well developed infrastructure and a share of agriculture that fluctuates around 15 per cent;

(3) agricultural regions, with a share of agriculture between 20 and 40 per cent and, apart from this, nothing else of any importance.[39]

Using this classification in relation to the provinces of the Netherlands, we run into a paradox. In 1970, in the 'semi-industrialised regions' of the Netherlands manufacturing had a much bigger share in the total GRP than in the 'industrialised regions' (see Table 6.4).

Table 6.4: Share of Manufacturing in GRP of Industrialised and Semi-industrialised Regions

Industrialised		Semi-industrialised	
Utrecht	29.03	Groningen	43.85
Noord-Holland	35.41	Zeeland	41.89
Zuid-Holland	38.11	Noord-Brabant	47.91
Gelderland	36.93	Limburg	43.82
		Overijssel	43.02

Source: See Table 6.3, p. 145.

It is difficult to fit Friesland and Drente into this scheme because they are the most markedly agricultural regions and their level of industrial activity is very low (see Table 6.3). So, obviously it is not the case that there are *no* industrial activities in the underdeveloped regions; on the contrary, the share of manufacturing is bigger there than elsewhere. But the questions remain what kind of industrial activities are there and what is their stage of development? This shows us once more that statistical structural indicators are, strictly speaking, inappropriate as representations of regional development. The need is more for indicators which make it possible to evaluate structure, stage and relative change of both production and size of labour force in their interconnection.

The same can be said for agriculture. The 'agricultural provinces' had small shares in the total of value produced in agriculture in 1970 (see Tables 6.2 and 6.5).

Table 6.5: Shares of Agricultural and Industrialised Regions in Agricultural Production

Agricultural		Industrialised	
Groningen	5.70	Zuid-Holland	16.68
Friesland	8.21	Noord-Holland	11.58
Drente	5.67		
Zeeland	5.19		

Source: See Table 6.3, p. 145.

The large share of both the Holland provinces indicates a very high productivity of labour, which is linked to the stage of integration of agriculture into the capitalist mode of production. Strictly speaking, one can not talk any more about agriculture *as a whole*. Market-gardening, stock-raising and arable farming (and even these are distinguished according to their various products) have their own dynamics of development within world market relations. In particular, developments in intensive stock-raising make the proportions of the 'agricultural regions' grow, so reducing the proportion of the West. The latter's high proportion is primarily accounted for by different forms of market-gardening.

The 'tertiary sector' or 'service sector' also encompasses a large variety of branches, each with its own dynamics of development. It is important to note that the 'tertiarisation' of the Dutch economy is not linked to the phasing out of industrial production, as is often suggested, but is closely related to the development of the productive forces. Table 6.2 shows this roughly: the high proportion of industry in the West is closely related to the even higher share of the service sector (the columns communication and transport and other firms). This is underlined by Table 6.6, in which the divisions of the number of employed people according to the different branches in the service sector are given for 1963.

Differences between the provinces in the retail trade and hotel and

Table 6.6: Employed Persons in Branches of the Service Sector as a Percentage of Total Employment, 1963

	Wholesale Trade	Retail Trade	Banking & Insurance	Transport & Communication	Hotel & Catering
Groningen	8	12	2	11	2
Friesland	8	14	3	7	3
Drente	6	12	2	6	3
Overijssel	6	10	1	5	2
Gelderland	7	11	2	6	3
Utrecht	8	13	4	8	3
N-Holland	10	13	6	11	3
Z-Holland	9	12	4	13	3
Zeeland	9	14	2	9	4
N-Brabant	6	10	2	4	2
Limburg	5	12	1	5	4
Netherlands	8	12	3	9	3

Source: CBS, Bedrijfstelling 1963, deel 3 regionale uitkomsten.

catering are slight. Both branches are directly orientated to the reproduction of the labour force and are therefore dependent on demographic characteristics. The remaining three branches (wholesale trade, banking and insurance, transport and communication) are closely related to the development of the productive forces. Clear nucleii can be found in the Randstad provinces (Utrecht and the Hollands). The growth of the service sector in Friesland and Drente (see Table 6.3) is mainly due to the rapid development of recreation. Without elaborating further, we wish to conclude by indicating the most important directions along which the interconnection between the development of the productive forces and the 'tertiary' sector has to be analysed:

(1) the change in the structure of production. In particular, its increasing scale and mass production and the consequent development in the sphere of circulation and in transport systems;
(2) the increasing socialisation of the reproduction of the labour force. This develops in two directions: first, a growing commercialisation of aspects of the reproduction of the labour force which were formerly in the realm of the family (e.g. catering, laundrettes). Second, an increasing number of aspects of reproduction are socially organised, especially by the state (e.g. education, health service);
(3) the scientisation of production or systematic application of science in the process of production (e.g. research and development, management).

As in the case of agriculture, so for the industrial and service sectors it is very important to analyse regional differentiation in a more detailed framework than that of the West and the rest of the Netherlands. Consequently developments have to be located more exactly than in the dual unity, centralisation — decentralisation, which is used in the bipolarity model. Each branch of activity in its spatial allocation is subject to a process of functional division of labour. Some aspects of this development of the functional division of labour in industry will now be presented.

Uneven and Heterogeneous Development of Regions

In an analysis of the development of industrial structure in the period 1930-50 Steigenga points to the fact that, although a relative loss of industrial employment in the West can be observed, it had a more than proportionate share (in terms of employment) in rapidly expanding industries which were tied to deep waterways. This geographical concentration was in contrast to a tendency towards decentralisation, mainly of industries tied to regional markets and the metal manufacturing and chemicals industries which were not tied to deep waterways. Selectivity could also be noticed in this process of decentralisation: the changes in the pattern of dispersal were not favourable to all provinces. For the agricultural provinces (Groningen, Friesland and Zeeland) this change even meant a decline in their relative position.[40]

In a review of regional aspects of the industrial structure of the Netherlands, Jansen and de Smidt concluded that 'on the basis of the characteristics of industrial movements, the tendencies towards centralisation were also selective after the Second World War' and that 'the distinction capital-intensity/labour-intensity is acceptable although broad.'[41] A comparison between the number of jobs created by the establishment of new firms during the period 1953-68 and the total increase in industrial employment then shows that in the West the former accounted for 25.6 per cent and the latter for 16.7 per cent hence 'the West might be characterised as the birthplace of a relatively large number of new firms, whereas extensions of [older] firms have been built mainly outside the West.'[42] These extensions have to be seen as expansions or subsidiaries of existing firms.

An indication of the selective character of the process of decentralisation of industry is given by a shift-and-share analysis of the development of employment which was done by Wever on the basis of the Censuses of Employment of 1950 and 1963.[43] The positive structural component of the Western provinces is clear. The relatively rapid

Table 6.7: Shift-and-Share Analysis of Industrial Employment Change, 1950-63

Province	Total shift (per cent)	Structural Component	Modification Component	Locational Component
Groningen	0.1	-2.8	2.7	0.2
Friesland	19.6	-6.3	4.2	21.7
Drente	54.0	-0.8	2.2	52.6
Overijssel	-9.0	-11.5	1.2	1.3
Gelderland	5.3	2.7	-2.5	5.1
Utrecht	-5.2	7.3	-3.4	-9.1
N-Holland	-12.4	2.0	0.1	-14.5
Z-Holland	-6.9	3.7	0.8	-11.4
Zeeland	-11.6	-6.4	3.9	-9.1
N-Brabant	12.7	-2.2	-2.1	17.0
Limburg	21.5	-0.0	2.8	18.7

Source: E. Wever, 'Enkele aspecten van industriele, ontwikkeling in Nederland tussen 1950 en 1963, *Nijmeegse Geografische Cahiers*, vol. 1 (1971).

growth of a number of provinces outside the West was adversely affected by the existing industrial structure and positively affected by locational factors in almost every case (Gelderland excluded). This technique of analysis provides the opportunity to establish statistically the relative similarities and differences in the development of regional structures compared to the national structure. However, only the degree of variation can be established. The calculated components say nothing about a possible explanation of developments. Primarily, they serve as a 'framework for further analysis'.[44]

An analysis, made by the Centraal Plan Bureau, of the factors which determined the tendencies of investment during the sixties concluded that 'there was the problem, at least in a rudimentary form, of a continuing tendency towards regional concentration. This was hindered, if not over-compensated for, by the constraining influence of the tight labour market in areas of concentration.'[45] Jansen and de Smidt pose the question of the *contents* of the processes by introducing the distinction between labour intensity and capital intensity. This distinction, however, is too broad.[46] For example, research into the migration of firms during the period 1950-62 shows that the North 'received' significantly less firms in clothing, textiles and food than the South and the East, but on the other hand significantly more metal manufacturing firms.[47] Hauer, Van der Knaap and de Smidt analysed changes in industrial structure during the sixties.[48] With the increase or decrease in the number of jobs by each industrial group during that particular period as background, they measured regional variations in degrees of increase or decrease in the industrial groups in question. By establishing the extent to which an industrial group was represented in a region as compared with the national average on two dates (30 June 1963 and 1968), they traced the effects of changes on the degree of representation of an industrial group in a region. Their central norm was the national growth rate of employment by industrial groups. The main problem with this method is that regional development is seen as national development in miniature. Particular historical, natural and social conditions are not integrated in this explanation.

From this review of the most relevant literature on the question of heterogeneous and uneven development of the Netherlands, we turn to three kinds of series based on the 'Regionale Rekeningen' (Regional Accounts) which have been assembled for the years 1960, 1965 and 1970. They are series in which (1) the level of, (2) the structure of, and (3) changes in provincial shares of industrial output and labour force are given. Tables 6.8 and 6.9 show the level of production measured in terms of shares of industrial output and labour force of certain industrial groups for 1960 and 1970. Tables 6.10 and 6.11 indicate changes in the shares. To complete this, Table 6.12 shows the structure of industrial production in terms of employment for the year 1970. Using the material compiled in these tables, the framework in which shifts in industrial structure took place can be outlined. The aggregation of various branches into industrial groups has been necessary because of the nature of the available data. The big disadvantage of this is that tendencies occurring within each of the particular branches cannot now be isolated and mutually reinforcing and constraining tendencies may be superimposed. For the interpretation of the developments contained in these tables an additional classification of industrial groups is desirable since structural changes in a region are highly determined by the character of production. A classification such as we use in this study is, strictly speaking, insufficient, but its problems cannot be dealt with in the context of this article. Hence as an expedient we have used the classification adopted by Hauer *et al.*[49] On the basis of the increase or decrease in employment, they proposed the following classification of industrial groups:

(1) chemicals and petroleum, metal manufacturing and engineering;
(2) food, drink and tobacco, timber and furniture, paper-making and printing;
(3) building material;
(4) leather and footwear, clothing;

Table 6.8: Shares of the Output of Industrial Groups by Province, 1960 and 1970

	Food, Drink Tobacco		Textiles		Leather, Clothing, Footwear		Timber, Furniture		Paper-making, Printing		Chemicals, Petroleum		Building Materials		Metal Manufacture, Engineering		Electricity, Transport		Construction	
	60	70	60	70	60	70	60	70	60	70	60	70	60	70	60	70	60	70	60	70
Groningen	6.30	4.73	0.86	1.86	4.01	4.16	5.10	5.57	6.96	7.22	3.14	8.14	3.10	4.66	2.50	2.58	2.35	2.97	4.02	3.46
Friesland	5.53	3.38	0.86	1.50	1.60	1.58	5.15	5.99	1.86	1.51	0.36	0.38	1.69	2.02	2.28	2.62	2.73	3.12	3.56	3.79
Drente	1.85	1.65	0.79	3.18	1.38	1.98	1.10	1.77	1.14	1.27	4.44	3.05	2.13	1.57	2.13	1.88	0.63	1.65	2.73	2.73
Overijssel	4.39	4.79	40.65	28.78	9.06	8.84	4.67	5.95	3.90	5.03	2.16	6.70	4.90	6.59	9.97	7.39	4.28	5.84	6.46	6.54
Gelderland	9.64	9.44	6.44	8.33	11.52	9.99	17.21	21.41	16.85	12.94	6.99	6.35	20.56	17.77	11.53	10.91	5.60	6.90	11.70	11.29
Utrecht	4.08	3.71	3.62	4.64	3.46	2.51	4.20	4.01	5.75	5.85	2.88	2.06	5.25	3.74	9.04	5.47	4.34	3.30	6.53	5.80
N-Holland	20.91	20.38	7.45	9.49	19.02	18.37	17.17	14.18	28.57	31.62	13.12	8.97	6.63	6.20	18.11	29.56	25.92	12.39	15.89	17.75
Z-Holland	25.36	26.67	5.45	4.59	16.53	7.47	25.15	19.15	19.72	18.62	49.76	44.47	20.38	20.65	26.18	22.67	23.67	23.22	25.05	25.81
Zeeland	1.59	1.45	1.22	1.79	0.81	1.49	1.06	1.00	0.62	0.53	2.67	5.44	2.22	3.63	0.40	1.13	1.83	2.37	3.65	2.70
N-Brabant	18.42	21.24	30.16	31.88	26.70	37.62	14.00	15.66	6.80	8.28	3.65	5.93	5.98	11.63	13.20	12.72	25.13	31.84	13.86	13.08
Limburg	2.45	2.54	2.49	4.00	5.91	6.00	4.09	5.30	7.72	7.14	10.64	8.58	27.16	21.59	4.66	6.26	4.52	6.41	7.11	7.09
Netherlands	100	100	100	100	100	100	100	100	100	100	100	100	100	100	100	100	100	100	100	100

Sources: Regionale Rekeningen 1965, CBS; Regionale Economische Indikatoren 1970, CBS.

Table 6.9: Shares of the Labour Force of Industrial Groups by Province, 1960 and 1970

	Food, Drink, Tobacco		Textiles		Leather, Clothing, Footwear		Timber, Furniture		Paper-making, Printing		Chemicals, Petroleum		Building Materials		Metal Manufacture, Transport, Engineering, Electricity		Construction	
	60	70	60	70	60	70	60	70	60	70	60	70	60	70	60	70	60	70
Groningen	4.78	4.34	1.07	2.03	4.62	5.66	5.25	4.66	7.23	6.67	3.64	2.74	3.58	3.33	3.09	3.28	4.06	3.54
Friesland	6.41	6.33	4.54	1.27	1.89	2.11	5.25	5.69	2.34	1.93	0.34	0.81	1.89	2.55	2.74	3.26	3.98	3.67
Drente	2.87	3.19	0.71	2.78	1.82	2.76	2.13	1.90	1.28	1.49	5.00	4.81	2.36	1.96	1.66	2.11	2.56	2.59
Overijssel	6.51	7.05	37.77	34.05	9.59	10.00	5.90	7.41	4.47	4.91	3.24	6.52	5.47	5.29	6.63	7.46	7.31	6.60
Gelderland	10.10	12.11	7.23	8.35	12.46	12.89	16.23	17.93	13.86	13.51	14.89	13.11	20.00	18.43	9.66	10.09	11.24	11.66
Utrecht	5.60	5.29	3.75	4.30	3.45	2.63	5.41	4.66	5.96	5.79	4.66	4.44	4.53	3.71	6.72	5.41	6.20	6.55
N-Holland	17.42	18.55	5.00	8.10	20.30	15.00	15.57	15.69	27.87	26.49	18.64	14.74	4.72	5.29	18.89	17.87	16.78	16.67
Z-Holland	22.20	20.72	4.91	4.43	12.69	7.76	23.20	27.93	27.55	21.05	26.93	27.11	22.08	21.96	25.24	21.50	24.70	23.56
Zeeland	1.77	1.87	1.88	1.52	1.11	1.32	1.48	1.21	0.74	0.70	2.61	3.04	2.45	2.75	1.73	1.85	2.80	3.02
N-Brabant	18.23	17.05	28.66	29.35	24.59	28.55	13.77	16.38	7.13	9.39	7.21	8.81	11.89	12.35	18.53	20.52	13.17	13.31
Limburg	4.11	3.55	3.13	3.80	7.48	11.32	5.79	6.55	6.60	8.07	12.84	13.85	21.13	22.35	5.41	6.65	7.12	6.85
Netherlands	100	100	100	100	100	100	100	100	100	100	100	100	100	100	100	100	100	100

Source: As Table 6.8.

(5) textiles.

The concrete course of processes of change in a region will not be considered in this analysis. For example, a relative increase in industry can take place because the development of the service sector fails to take place, the productive forces stagnate in their development, the existing productive machinery is extended quantitatively, new firms from the Randstad move in or agriculture is rapidly rationalised and restructured. It is, however, possible to elucidate some aspects of changes in the industrial structure of the various provinces:

Table 6.10: Changes in Provincial Shares of Industrial Output, 1960-1970

	Food, Drink, Tobacco	Textiles	Leather, Footwear, Clothing	Timber, Furniture	Paper-making, Printing	Chemicals, Petroleum	Building Materials	Metal Manufacture, Engineering	Electricity, Transport, Others	Construction
Groningen	−	+	o	o	o	++	+	o	+	−
Friesland	−	+	o	+	o	o	o	o	o	−
Drente	o	+	+	+	o	−	−	o	+	o
Overijssel	o	−−	o	+	+	++	+	−−	+	−
Gelderland	o	++	−	++	−−	−	−	−−	+	o
Utrecht	o	+	−	o	o	−	−	−−	−	+
N-Holland	−	+	−	−−	++	−−	o	++	−−	−
Z-Holland	+	−	−−	−−	−	−−	o	−−	+	−
Zeeland	o	+	+	o	o	++	+	+	+	+
N-Brabant	++	+	++	+	+	+	++	−	++	++
Limburg	o	++	o	+	−	−	−−	+	+	−

Explanation of the signs:
　　−− < − 2.5%
− 2.5 < − < − 0.5
− 0.5 < o < 　0.5
0.5 < + < 2.5
2.5 < ++
Source: As Table 6.8.

(1) A clear shift has taken place in the economic structure of the northern (Friesland, Groningen, Drente) and the southern (Noord-Brabant, Limburg) provinces, in the sense that textiles, leather and footwear and timber and furniture are becoming more important. This involves branches of industry which can be characterised as

Table 6.11: Changes in Provincial Shares of Industrial Labour Force, 1960-70

	Food, Drink, Tobacco	Textiles	Leather, Footwear, Clothing	Timber, Furniture	Paper-making, Printing	Chemicals, Petroleum	Building Materials	Metal Manufacture, Engineering, Electricity, Transport	Construction
Groningen	o	+	+	−	−	−	o	o	−
Friesland	o	+	o	o	o	o	+	o	o
Drente	o	+	+	o	o	o	o	o	o
Overijssel	+	−−	o	+	o	++	o	+	−
Gelderland	+	+	o	+	o	−	−	o	o
Utrecht	o	+	−	−	o	o	−	+	o
N-Holland	+	++	−−	o	−	−−	+	−	o
Z-Holland	−	o	−−	−−	−	+	o	−−	+
Zeeland	o	o	o	o	o	o	o	o	o
N-Brabant	−	+	++	++	+	+	o	+	o
Limburg	−	+	++	+	+	+	+	+	o

Explanation of the signs:

$−− < −2.5\%$
$−2.5 < − < −0.5$
$−0.5 < o < 0.5$
$0.5 < + < 2.5$
$2.5 < ++$

Source: As Table 6.8

weak in respect of both their labour productivity and the number of jobs.

(2) The big concentration of negative signs (Tables 6.10 and 6.11) for the western provinces points to the process of 'tertiarisation'. The large number of positive signs for Limburg and Noord-Brabant indicates that here there has been a more general process of development in industry, not simply increased concentration of 'weak' branches of production.

(3) in certain cases a big increase in shares of output does not correspond with the direction of the sign of changes in employment. This is the case in Groningen with chemicals, paper-making and printing, and timber and furniture. A comparison between the output/employment ratio for these industrial groups by province (as an indicator of the productivity of labour) and the national average shows us that this is a case where the increase of labour productivity exceeds the national average.

(4) For textiles, leather and footwear as well as for chemicals and

petroleum, there appears to be a relationship between above-average increases in the productivity of labour and their increasing import-ance in the regional structure of production, measured in terms of employment.

(5) In relation to chemicals and petroleum, the dynamism of devel-opment has to be stressed. The shares by province vary considerably. Furthermore, it is a very heterogeneous industrial group, in which traditional industries like soap and detergents, which are often small, exist alongside the monopolistic petrochemicals industry.[50]

With Table 6.12 we provisionally complete the picture of changes in industrial structure. It reflects the relative strengths or weaknesses of the various industrial groups by comparing provincial and national shares. It is clear that not only are various weak groups strongly repre-sented but also a number of 'growth industries' (like chemicals and, to a lesser extent, metal manufacturing and paper-making and printing) under-represented in the border provinces.

Thus far we have been concerned with data on structure. *Overall shifts in structure take place through cyclical movements.* It has been briefly noted that tendencies in spatial development can be reinforced by tendencies of increased over-accumulation and the allied tendency of the profit rate to fall, as has become apparent in the recent crisis cycles. Without being able to deal with these exhaustively, we want to make some comments on them in the next sections.

Cyclical Movements

The development of the national cycle can be seen as a resultant of the interdependent cycles of the various branches of industry. The charac-teristic of the current period is that the cycles of these branches are becoming increasingly heterogeneous. On the one hand, there are branches which have run into serious problems (shipbuilding, textiles), and, on the other, there are branches which are expanding rapidly (parts of chemicals, electronics).[51] This heterogeneity has to be considered as an expression of further integration into the world market, whereas at the level of the world market national cycles are becoming more homogeneous.

As regards the relationship between uneven development of branches of industry and uneven regional development, we have limited ourselves so far to regional structure through an analysis of the regional division of labour. The question of *development* will now be discussed. We will examine one of the indicators of the development of the industrial

Table 6.12: Provincial Share of Industrial Groups in Employment, 1970

	Food, Drink Tobacco	Textiles	Leather Footwear, Clothing	Timber, Furniture	Paper-making, Printing	Chemicals, Petroleum	Building Materials	Metal Manufacture, Engineering	Construction
Groningen	12.10	2.69	5.54	• 6.22	•• 12.77	6.22	2.86	o 25.38	26.22
Friesland	•• 20.11	1.92	3.07	• 6.32	o 4.21	oo 2.11	2.49	28.74	• 31.03
Drente	12.93	•• 5.37	5.12	2.68	o 4.15	•• 15.85	2.44	oo 23.66	27.80
Overijssel	8.93	•• 20.53	5.80	3.28	o 4.27	6.72	2.06	o 26.18	oo 22.21
Gelderland	10.74	3.53	5.24	5.56	8.23	9.46	5.02	o 24.79	27.46
Utrecht	10.22	4.00	2.35	3.07	7.76	7.05	2.23	29.26	•• 33.96
N-Holland	11.57	o 2.40	4.28	3.42	• 11.34	7.84	1.01	30.88	•• 27.61
Z-Holland	10.19	o 1.04	o 1.75	3.08	7.11	10.89	3.32	29.30	•• 33.38
Zeeland	9.09	3.52	2.93	2.05	o 2.35	• 12.51	4.11	o 24.44	•• 39.00
N-Brabant	10.69	• 8.76	8.20	3.59	o 4.04	o 4.50	2.38	•• 35.66	oo 22.18
Limburg	oo 4.86	o 2.47	7.80	3.13	7.58	•• 15.40	•• 9.39	o 25.21	o 24.88
Netherlands	10.51	5.00	4.81	3.67	7.22	8.54	3.23	29.11	27.91

Explanation of the signs
Strongly represented • > 2.5 per cent above the national share
                     •• > 5 per cent " " " " " "
Weakly represented   o > 2.5 per cent below the national share
                    oo > 5 per cent " " " " " "

Source: As Table 6.8.

cycle, namely investment in fixed assets by provinces. As has been noted, these data only reflect development; they do not give an insight into the determining factor of spatial structure — the development of fixed capital, in its quantitative and qualitative dimensions. Table 6.13 shows the distribution of investment in fixed industrial assets by provinces and major regions while Figure 6.3 shows the cyclical sensitivity of the northern provinces. Movements in the cycle take place there much sooner than in the other major regions of the country.

Table 6.13: Shares in Investment in Fixed Assets in Manufacturing Industry, 1968-75

	1968	1969	1970	1971	1972	1973	1974	1975
Groningen	4.35	4.04	3.69	2.93	3.59	4.43	4.58	4.17
Friesland	2.46	2.22	2.14	2.13	2.21	2.59	2.85	2.27
Drente	2.62	2.46	2.98	1.92	1.57	2.03	2.88	2.30
Overijssel	5.12	5.01	5.16	4.65	4.87	6.26	6.77	5.71
Gelderland	7.57	8.49	8.58	7.65	8.33	8.31	8.96	8.52
Utrecht	3.38	3.59	3.60	3.45	3.12	3.89	4.11	3.65
N-Holland	22.32	20.51	18.21	17.66	16.38	12.24	14.90	16.21
Z-Holland	28.53	25.54	24.27	25.93	23.51	18.32	17.16	24.02
Zeeland	5.70	7.16	8.71	7.86	9.20	8.98	5.25	6.13
N-Brabant	11.91	13.28	13.60	16.18	20.76	24.36	22.53	16.60
Limburg	6.04	7.26	8.55	9.60	6.44	8.58	10.30	10.43
North	9.43	8.72	8.76	6.98	7.37	9.05	10.31	8.74
East	12.69	13.50	13.74	12.30	13.30	14.57	15.73	14.23
West	54.23	49.64	46.15	47.09	43.01	34.45	36.17	43.88
South	23.65	27.70	30.86	33.64	36.40	41.92	37.78	33.16

Source: CBS, Statistiek Investeringen in vaste aktiva in de nijverheid 1968, 1969-75

An evaluation of data such as that shown in Table 6.13 led the Centraal Plan Bureau to conclude that the North showed

the strongest tendency to fall behind in various cycles, i.e. usually more than 10 per cent below the national average. The difference is something less than 10 per cent for the East and under 5 per cent for the South. The West, however, shows a smaller fall and keeps investing 5 per cent more than the national average. For the service sector, it is not possible to identify a clear regional cyclical picture as above.[52]

Sensitivity is greater in the North, but the amplitude of the movement is less than in the West and the South. Possible reasons could be: (1)

Figure 6.3: Investment in Fixed Assets in Manufacturing Industry by Major Regions, 1968-75

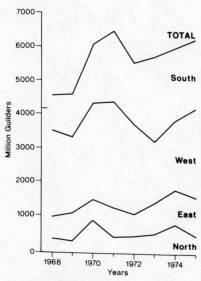

shifts in the cycle are dependent on the scale of investment. Certain (replacement) investments always have to be undertaken so, crisis or not, investment cannot fall below a certain minimum; (2) the nature of the structure of production, the composition of the branches of industry; (3) activities of 'supra-regional' firms can have a dampening influence on amplitude: their investment decisions are only dependent to a small degree on the local situation. However, the converse can also be the case: in a period of restructuring of the production process, monopolies often first reorganise at their subsidiaries in 'peripheral' areas; (4) finally subsidies and other forms of public expenditure can have a dampening influence. Despite the fact that the effects of regional policy have been shown to be very limited, this state intervention has to be further analysed in relation to the process of 'filtering down'.

A more detailed insight into Figure 6.3 is obtained by relating it to the cycles of investment in some important industrial groups and to industrial structure. In particular, the large share of investment in the metal manufacturing and chemicals and petroleum industries in the West and South is reflected by the similarity between Figures 6.4 and 6.5 and the curves for the South and West in Figure 6.3. After a big increase in the North during the years 1969-70, a sharp decline in investment took place in the following year with reductions in

Figure 6.4: Investment in Fixed Assets in Metal Manufacturing, 1964-75

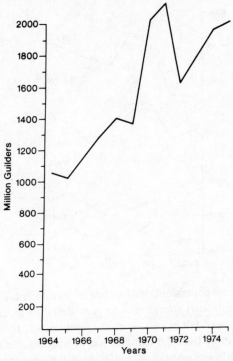

chemicals, food, drink and tobacco, building material and — to a lesser extent — metal manufacturing. The first three accounted for more than 65 per cent of all investment in this region. This sharp decline differs from the relative stability of national development and was the fore-runner of a more general recession. The increase in investment in the South is entirely accounted for by the chemicals industry in Noord-Brabant: 100 in 1970 and 580 in 1971. Without Shell Moerdijk the same picture as in the West and the East would have been created. The decline in 1971-2 was most clearly expressed in the West, especially in the metal manufacturing and chemical industries. A large decline also occurred in the South, except in metal manufacturing and chemicals. During 1972-3, investment rose everywhere except in the Randstad. One can see this in the graph for chemicals and petroleum. Because investment in chemicals in Limburg rose, this relative loss of investment was accentuated for the Randstad. During 1974-5 another clear cyclical shift can be noted in the North and the East, in contrast to the South,

Figure 6.5: Investment in Fixed Assets in the Chemical and Petroleum Industries, 1964-75

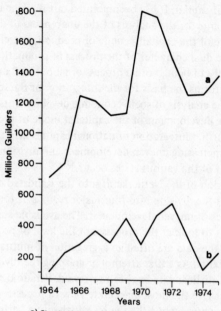

a) Chemical Industry, including starch-derivates, synthetic yarns and fibres
b) Petroleum Industry, excluding petro-chemicals

where an increase occurred in those branches of industry which declined in the North and East.

Summary Remarks

The structure of a region is not a miniature copy of the national socio-economic structure. The development of regions has to be analysed in terms of the interrelated processes of functional and spatial division of labour. Regional economics based on the neo-classical theory of equilibrium denies regional uneven development as a problem by its assumptions. Modern location theory starts from the unevenness of regional development but does not grasp the interrelationship between the various processes of creation and development of areas of concentration, of declining regions and of undeveloped or hardly developed regions. Among Marxist contributions, the explanation of regional uneven development in highly developed capitalist countries draws on the analytical models of imperialism. We have indicated why this is incorrect.

An explanation of regional uneven development within highly advanced countries has to start from the internal laws of development and functioning of capital. It has been pointed out that the methodological starting-points for the analysis of the unevenness of development lie in the structure of the capitalist mode of production itself. The recognition of the dual character of the process of production as a contradictory unity of being both a process of labour and a process of value creation forms the basis for the integration of the spatial dimension into the analysis of socio-economic developments.

Along with the development of the capitalist mode of production and the related further integration of national capitals into the world market, steadily increasing uneven development and division of labour within the regions of the various states occur.[53]

The usual division of the Netherlands into the Randstad and the rest of the country, or the division into four major regions, is too broad to grasp the processes of uneven development. The available statistical material forced us to look at the processes at the level of provinces. Even at this level the data are often an aggregation of mutually contradictory developments. As a first attempt at grasping the diversity, part of the available statistical data has been reviewed. Paradoxically, the most exact figures give the most inaccurate view of processes of change of the regional structure, while the figures which give a better reflection of the actual changes in the socio-economic structure of regions are less accurate.

A number of aspects of uneven development have not been considered in this chapter and much work has yet to be done in order to understand the essence and forms of appearance of regional development. If this chapter can make a contribution to discussion about the theoretical and empirical aspects of regional unevenness and thus a contribution to the removal of unevenness in opportunities for development of people, then it has fulfilled its function.

Notes

1. Our argument here relates to Marxist contributions. Traditional theories of spatial economics, based on neo-classical equilibrium theory, disregard the problem of uneven spatial development because of their theoretical assumptions. In contributions from 'polarisation-theories' developed in the wake of Myrdal's critique of the balanced growth theorem, the differences in development between peripheral and central regions are elaborated but not systematically explained.

2. Two important contributions which are not based on the theories of the 'transfer of value' and 'dependencia' are Felix Damette's essay, 'The Regional

Framework of Monopoly Exploitation' (Chapter 4 here) and M.R. Andreola, C. Capitani, P. Laureano and G. Paba, 'La redistributione multinazionale della attivita produttive: verso una nuova geografia della forze lavoro', *Quaderni del Territorio*, no. 1 (1976). At this stage of our research we cannot, however, go further into these contributions but for a critique of Damette's position see P. van Hoogstraten, 'Aanzetten voor een kritiek op Damette', *Zone*, no. 4 (1977).

3. For a critical review of the thesis of the 'transfer of value' see the work of Klaus Busch, *Die Multinationalen Konzerne – zur Analyse der Weltmarkt bewegung Reproduktion des Kapitals* (Frankfurt a.m., 1974) and W. Schöller, *Weltmarkt und Reproduction des Kapitals* (Frankfurt/Köln, 1976). For a critical reassessment of the 'dependencia' discussions, see, *inter alia*, T. Hurtiennee, 'Zur Ideologiekritik der Latein-amerikanischen Theorien der Unterwentwicklung und Abhängigkeit', *Probleme des Klassenkampfes*, nos. 14/15 (1974).

4. As references to both types of contribution we can cite:

(1) the discussion on regional underdevelopment based on the theory of the 'transfer of value' in D. Belmann *et al.*, 'Provinz als Politisches Problem', especially Part 3, 'Ansatze zu einer Theorie der "Provinz", Ungleiche Entwicklung im Kapitalismus', *Kursbuch*, no. 39 (1975). In the Netherlands an 'exploitation relation' between, for example, the North and the Randstad is often referred to without elaboration and explicit argumentation.

(2) The discussion based on 'dependencia' in A. Evers, 'Fragen an eine korrigierte Raumpolitik', *Stadtbauwelt* (1975) and G. Duyf, *Ongelijke ontwikkeling in Nederland: een inventariserend onderzoek naar de verschijningsvormen van regionalee ontwikkeling* (Tilburg, 1977).

5. The main weakness of this contribution becomes clear here: only the process of underdevelopment *between* different national states is discussed. The question of uneven development *within* national capitals is either excluded or partially explained as a result of the *modification* of the law of value but not by the internal laws of development of capital. As regards the thesis of the 'transfer of value', we can briefly note that the permanent transfer of value from 'peripheral areas' to 'centres', which is supposed to be the cause of underdevelopment, is theoretically only tenable when it is limited to transfer of value between sectors with different relations of production, i.e. between capitalist and non-capitalist sectors.

6. This division in the analysis is largely the result of the requirements of a systematic explanation. Of course, it is obvious that systematic development of theory is only possible on the basis of research into the real, historical processes of development. On the other hand, these processes can only be analysed when they can be reduced to the laws of the development and functioning of social processes. In the postface to the second edition of Volume One of *Capital*, Marx explains the relation between the method of inquiry and the method of presentation as follows:

> Of course the method of representation must differ in form from that of inquiry. The latter has to appropriate the material in detail, to analyse its different forms of development and to trace down their inner connection. Only after this work has been done can the real movement be approximately represented. If this is done successfully, if the life of the subject matter is now reflected back in the ideas, then it may appear as if we have before us an *a priori* construction (*Capital* (Pelican edition, Penguin Books, Harmondsworth, 1976), vol. 1, p. 102 (*Marx-Engels Werke* (*MEW*), 23, p. 27)).

7. In the context of this article we cannot go further into the historical pro-

cesses of development in the dynamics of capital accumulation. Since the basic spatial structure that was created during the Industrial Revolution has essentially influenced the subsequent processes of development and restructuring, a great deal of emphasis should be placed on this stage in the development of capitalism as the process of accumulation tends to reproduce existing spatial agglomerations.

8. J. Huffschmid, 'Begrundung und Bedeutung des Monopolbegiffs in der marxischten politischen Oekonomie', *Das Argument Sonderband*, no. 6 (West Berlin, 1975).

9. Cf. the explanation given by K.H. Tjaden, 'Die räumliche Ungleichmässigkeit gesellschaftlicher Entwicklung als theoretisches Problem', *18th Meeting of German Sociologists (Soziologentag)* (Bielefeld, 1975).

10. See K.H. Marx, *Capital*, vol. 1, pp. 472-3 (*MEW*, 23, p. 374).

11. Cf. Karl Wittfogel's essay on the meaning of the natural moment in the development of social production in 'Geopolitik, geographischer Materialismus und Marximus', *Unter dem Banner des Marxismus*, Heft 1, p. 17; Heft 4, p. 458ff. and Heft 5, p. 698ff. (1929, Reprint, Erlangen, 1970).

12. See Felix Damette's essay (pp. 76-92 above) where he writes about the closures of firms in the Pas-de-Calais region and the development of new production complexes in the Basse-Seine region. The changes in the raw materials used as feedstock for chemicals production in the Netherlands, from coal to natural gas and naptha, meant the removal of a complete regional structure of production in the south of Limburg, an enormous expansion of the seaport complex around Rotterdam and the development of a completely new production complex in Zeeland.

13. For the increase in productivity (productive power) of social labour through co-operation and division of labour see Marx, *Capital*, vol. 1, p. 446 and p. 486 (*MEW*, 23, p. 348ff and p. 386).

14. For a discussion of the 'costless character' of natural forces see Marx, *Capital*, vol. 1, p. 508 (*MEW*, 23, p. 407).

15. This is one of the main causes of the actual decline of employment in industrial production. As will be indicated later, this decline of employment is usually connected with an expansion of other sectors, which are referred to by the unspecific notion 'tertiary sector'.

16. In his exposition on 'co-operation and manufacture', Marx shows how the 'combined collective labourer' is developed by the capitalist form of development of productivity — initially at the level of the firm. The 'combined collective labourer' is the result of the systematic division and specialisation of functions within a firm into ever more one-sided, detailed activities which are combined into one complete mechanism of production under the command of capital. This process of systematic socialisation of production, however, is not limited to the level of the firm alone. The intentional technical application of science in production evolves in relation to the processes of centralisation and concentration of capital. At the same time, this leads to an enormous reorganisation of total social labour, to a 'progressive transformation of isolated processes of production, carried on by customary methods, into socially combined and scientifically arranged processes of production' (Marx, *Capital*, vol. 1, p. 780, *MEW*, 23, p. 656). The social collective labourer assumes more and more the character of a 'combined collective labourer' with one principal limitation in every case. Because of private capitalist relations of production, this combination is not achieved by way of conscious planning but as an uncontrollable result of spontaneous market processes.

17. We cannot elaborate here on the functions of the state as they result from the antagonism between increasing socialisation and the capitalist organisation of production but see, *inter alia*, Dieter Läpple's essay, 'Kapitalistische Vergesellschaftungstendenzen und Staatsinterventionismus' in V. Brandes (ed.), *Handbuch*

5: Staat (Frankfurt/Köln, 1977).

18. Cf. H. Bömer,'Internationale Kapitalskonzentration und regionale Krise-neutwicklung am Beispiel der Montanindustrie under der Montanregionen der Europäischen Gemeinschaft' (unpublished PhD thesis, Dortmund, 1975) and R. Bönisch *et al.*, *Territorialplaning* (East Berlin, 1976).

19. By tendencies of decentralisation, we refer only to large-scale tendencies and not to those which are regionally limited and which result from problems and conflicts related to the use of space within urban agglomerations. An example is the relocation of industries to the outer fringes of urban areas because of require-ments resulting from industrial expansion itself or from processes of suburbanisa-tion which mainly result from the pursuit of higher living standards by high-and middle-income groups.

20. Cf. DATAR, *Investments étrangers et Aménagement du Territoire* (Livre Blanc, Paris, 1974); M. Benetti, M. Ferrara and C. Medori, *Il Capitale Strangiero nel Mezzogiorno* (Coines Edizioni, 1975); J. Firn, 'External Control and Regional Policy' in G. Brown (ed.), *Red Paper on Scotland* (EUSPB, Edinburgh, 1975), pp. 153-69; S. Holland, 'Multinational Companies and a Selective Regional Policy', House of Commons Expenditure Committee, Session 1972-3, *Regional Development Incentives* (HMSO, London, 1973), vol. II; W. Cremers, 'Regionalafhankelijkheid door nevenvestigingen', in Projektgroep Regional Onderontwikkeling, *Een Kwart eeuw overheidsbeleid* (Rijks Universiteit, Socio-logies Institut, Groningen, 1975); A. Gorz, *Le Socialisme difficile – Colonialisme dedans et dehors* (Editions du Seuil, Paris, 1967), Ch. 5.

21. The title of the first White Paper on physical planning in the Netherlands, dating from 1958, is typical: 'Het Westen en Overig Nederland' ('The West and the Rest of the Netherlands').

22. J.H. Pirie, 'Het Verval van de Randstad', *Intermediair*, no. 5 (1976).

23. J. Lambooy and H.J. Huizinga, 'Het Nieuwe Westen, balans van 20 jaar ontwikkeling', *Intermediair*, no. 12 (1967).

24. F.J. Gay, 'Benelux' in H.D. Clout (ed.), *Regional Development in Western Europe* (Wiley, London, 1975), p. 151.

25. Lambooy and Huizinga, 'Het Nieuwe Westen', p. 3.

26. Centraal Plan Bureau (CPB), *Centraal Economisch Plan 1978* (Den Haag, 1978), p. 264.

27. Ibid.

28. Ibid.

29. A.C. Janssen and M. de Smidt, *Industrie en Ruimte; de industriele ont-wikkeling van Nederland in een veranderend sociaal-ruimtelijk bestel* (Assen, 1974), p. 22.

30. Cf. H. Roland Holst, *Kapital en Arbeid in Nederland* (2 vols., 1902 and 1937, SUN Reprint, Nijmegen, 1972); J.A. de Jonge, *De industrialisatie in Neder-land tussen 1950 en 1954* (SUN Reprint, Nijmegen, 1976); P. Offermans and B. Feis, *Geschiedenis van het gewone volk van Nederland* (SOF, Nijmegen, 1975).

31. Cf. H.J. Keuning, *Het Nederlandse Volk in zijn woongebied* (Leopold, Den Haag, 1947).

32. P. van Hoogstraten and N. Kentgens, 'De Mijnstreek: enkele aspekten van regionale outwikkeling', *Zone*, no. 1 (1976), pp. 8-99.

33. On the 'big increase of Dutch exports and the increasing penetration of imported goods' see *Nota Inzake de Selective Groei* (Den Haag, 1976), p. 223ff.

34. Jansen and de Smidt, *Industrie en Ruimte, p. 31ff.*

35. Cf. H. Claussen and D. Läpple, *Regionaluntersuchung Bremen: Regional-analytische Rahmenuntersuchung für die Erforschung von Belastungsschwer-punkten von Lohnabhangigen am Arbeitzplatz under Arbeitsumgebung* (Bremen, 1976).

36. Ibid., p. 8.

37. Ibid., p. 10ff.

38. W. de Wreede, 'Een Valuatie van de Bruikfaarheid van Officiele Statistieken', in *Economisch Statistische Berichten*, vol. 7, no. 6 (1978).

39. Commission of the European Community, *A Regional Policy for the Community* (Brussels, 1969), p. 14 ff.

40. W. Steigenga, 'De decentralistatie van de Nederlandse industrie, een economisch-geograpfische en statistische analyse van de veranderingen in het spreidings-patroon der industriele werkgelegenheid in de periode 1930-1950', *Tijdschrift voor Economische en Sociale Geografie* (TESG), vol. 49 (1958), p. 129ff.

41. Jansen and De Smidt, *Industrie en Ruimte*, p. 72.

42. J. Hauer, G.A. van der Knaap and M. de Smidt, 'Changes in the Industrial Geography of the Netherlands during the sixties', *TESG*, vol. 62 (1971), p. 146.

43. E. Wever, 'Enkele aspecten van industriele ontwikkeling in Nederland tussen 1950 en 1963, *Nijmeegse Geografische Cahiers*, vol. 1 (1971).

44. T.W. Buck, quoted by Wever, 'Enkele aspecten', p. 24. See also J.H. Muller, *Methoden zur regionalen Analyse und Prognose* (Schroedel Verlag, Hanover, 1976), p. 71.

45. CPB, *De Nederlandse economie in 1980* (Den Haag, 1976), p. 238.

46. In the rest of their argument, they try to reduce this breadth by analysing industrial interrelationships in a geographical perspective through the introduction of so-called 'industrial formations'. Here the emphasis is especially laid on internal and external 'economies of scale'. The formations are looked at separately (seaport formation, urban formation) and not in terms of their interrelationship.

47. SISWO, *Verplaatsing van Industriele Bedrijvendeelraport 1* (Amsterdam, 1967).

48. Hauer *et al.*, 'Industrial Geography', p. 137ff.

49. The classification has to be slightly changed because of another combination of branches into industrial groups.

50. The conclusions which we have drawn from the tables are not exhaustive. At the current stage of our research this is not yet possible. The analysis of inter-regional relationships and the analysis of developments in the various branches of industry are mutually reinforcing.

51. CPB, *De Nederlandse economie*, p. 141. Recently the CPB announced that the economic recession had caused an exacerbation of the unevenness of development in individual branches of industry; cf. CPB, *Centraal Economisch Plan*, p. 15ff.

52. CPB, *De Nederlandse economie*, p. 225.

53. CPB, *Centraal Economisch Plan*, p. 284: 'In the current period of stagnation, regional differences have *again* become aggravated.' Where that 'again' comes from is not clear because this is the first time that it has been officially stated that these processes occur. The euphoria of the Dutch about planning always led to its denial.

7 FURTHER READING

The purpose of this chapter is to identify further books and articles which have contributed to the establishment of new perspectives in European regional theory. The first section contains references dealing with theoretical issues raised in previous chapters and the second with regional case studies.

Theory

Modes of Production and their Articulation

In constructing an interpretation of regional problems, Alain Lipietz, in part, deploys an Althusserian vocabulary. This is comprehensively set out in: L. Althusser, *For Marx* (Penguin, Harmondsworth, 1969); L. Althusser and E. Balibar, *Reading Capital* (New Left Books, London, 1970); B. Hindess and P.Q. Hirst, *Pre-Capitalist Modes of Production* (Routledge and Kegan Paul, London, 1975) and B. Hindess and P.Q. Hirst, *Mode of Production and Social Formation* (Macmillan, London, 1977). A powerful critique of Althusserian propositions is put forward in E.P. Thompson's book, *The Poverty of Theory and Other Essays* (Merlin, London, 1978).

On the articulation of modes of production, see S. Amin, 'Accumulation and Development', *Review of African Political Economy*, vol. 1 (1974), pp. 9-26; S. Amin, *Unequal Development* (Harvester, Lewes, Sussex, 1977); J. Friedman, 'Tribes, States and Transformations' in M. Bloch (ed.), *Marxist Analysis and Social Anthropology* (Malbay, London, 1975); M. Godelier, *Rationality and Irrationality in Economics* (New Left Books, London, 1972); P.P. Rey, 'The Lineage Mode of Production', *Critique of Anthropology*, no. 3 (1975), pp. 27-79; and P.P. Rey, *Les Alliances des Classes* (Maspero, Paris, 1973).

The regional articulation of modes of production is analysed in M.V. Cabral, 'Agrarian Structures and Recent Rural Movements in Portugal', *Journal of Peasant Studies*, vol. 5 (1978), pp. 411-45 and F. da C. Medeiros, 'Capitalisme et Précapitalisme dans les campagnes portugaises de l'entre-deux-guerres', *Etudes Rurales*, vol. 67 (1977), pp. 7-29.

Alain Lipietz's views are set out more fully in his book *Le Capital et Son Espace* (Maspero, Paris, 1977). His most recent work analyses the service sector in France; see, for example, his paper, 'La Dimension Régionale du Developpement du Tertiaire', *Centre d'Etudes Prospectives d'Economie Mathématique Appliquée à la Planification*, no. 7801 (1978). M. Blondeau reviews *Le Capital et Son Espace* in his article 'Un Nouvel Eclairage: "Le Capital et son Espace" d'Alain Lipietz', *Espaces-Temps*, nos. 10-11 (1979), pp. 66-71.

Spatial Division of Labour

On the inter-regional division of labour, see J. Carney, J. Lewis and R. Hudson, 'Coal Combines and Inter-regional Uneven Development in the UK' and J.-P. Laurençin, J-C. Monateri, C. Palloix, R. Tiberghien and P. Vernet, 'The Regional Effects of the Crisis on the Forms of Organisation of Production and Location of Industry in the Mediter-ranean Basin' in D.B. Massey and P.W.J. Batey (eds.), *Alternative Frameworks for Analysis* (Pion, London, 1977), pp. 52-67 and 7-18 respectively; D.B. Massey, 'Regionalism: Some Current Issues', *Capital and Class*, no. 6 (1978), pp. 106-25; D.B. Massey, 'In What Sense a Regional Problem?', *Regional Studies* (forthcoming, 1979); C. Michon-Savarit, 'La place des régions françaises dans la division internationale du travail: deux scénarios contrastés', *Environment and Planning*, A, vol. 7, no. 4 (1975), pp. 449-54; F. Olivera and H.P. Reichstul, 'Mudanças na divisão interregional do trabalho no Brazil', *Ciência e Cultura*, vol. 26, no. 3 (1974), pp. 225-39; and B. Secchi, 'Central and Peripheral Regions in a Process of Economic Development: the Italian Case' in Massey and Batey, *Alternative Frameworks*, pp. 36-51.

A major recent study of changes in the international division of labour is the book by F. Frobel, J. Heinrichs and O.K. Rowolt, *Die Neue Internationale Arbeitsteillung* (Reinbek bei, Hamburg, 1977). The main findings are summarised in F. Frobel, J. Heinrichs and D. Kreye, 'The Tendency Towards a New International Division of Labour', *Economic and Political Weekly*, vol. 11, nos. 5-7 (1976), pp. 159-70; see also S. Hymer, 'The Multinational Corporation and the Law of Uneven Development' in J.N. Bhagwati (ed.), *Economics and World Order* (Orient Longman Ltd, 1972), pp. 113-40, reprinted in H. Radice (ed.), *International Firms and Modern Imperialism* (Penguin, Harmondsworth, 1975), pp. 37-62; R. Murray, 'Underdevelopment, International Firms and the International Division of Labour' in *Towards a New World Economy* (Rotterdam University Press, Rotter-dam, 1972), pp. 161-247; D. Nayyar, 'Transnational Corporations and Manufactured Exports from Poor Countries', *Economic Journal*, vol. 88 (1978) and B. Stuckey, 'The Spatial Distribution of the Industrial

Reserve Army', *Zone Werkkongres* (Amsterdam, May 1977).

The State

For a general review of current theories of the State see B. Jessop, 'Recent Theories of the Capitalist State', *Cambridge Journal of Economics*, vol. 1 (1977), pp. 353-73. Laclau discusses the views of Poulantzas and Miliband in his article, 'The Specificity of the Political', *Economy and Society*, vol. 4 (1975), pp. 87-110; see also N. Poulantzas 'The Capitalist State: a Reply to Miliband and Laclau', *New Left Review*, no. 95 (1976), pp. 63-83.

The theory of State fiscal crisis tendencies was first put forward by James O'Connor in his book *The Fiscal Crisis of the State* (Saint Martin's Press, New York, 1973) and is further discussed in Ian Gough's article, 'State Expenditure in Advanced Capitalism', *New Left Review*, no. 92 (1975), pp. 53-92.

The German debate on the State is reflected in J. Holloway and S. Picciotto (eds.), *State and Capital* (Arnold, London, 1978). Offe's article, 'The Theory of the Capitalist State and the Problem of Policy Formation', is also crucial. It is found in L.N. Lindberg, R. Alford, C. Crouch and C. Offe (eds.), *Stress and Contradiction in Modern Capitalism* (D.C. Heath, Farnborough, 1975), pp. 125-44.

The relationships between the State, regional problems and local society are discussed in: D. Bleitrach and A. Chenu, 'Aménagement: régulation ou aggravation des contradictions sociales? Un example: Fos-sur-mer et l'aire métropolitaine marseillaise', *Environment and Planning*, A, vol. 7, no. 4 (1975), pp. 367-91; D. Bleitrach, 'Région métropolitaine et appareils hégémoniques locaux', *Espaces et Sociétés* (1977), pp. 47-65; R. Dulong, 'La crise du rapport Etat/société locale vue au travers de la politique régional' in N. Poulantzas (ed.), *La crise de l'Etat* (PUF, Paris, 1976), pp. 209-32; R. Dulong, *Les régions, l'Etat et la Société locale* (PUF, Paris, 1978) and J. Lévy, 'Pour une problématique: Région et formation économique et sociale', *Espaces Temps*, nos. 10-11 (1979), pp. 80-107.

Crisis

The current international recession is analysed in Ernest Mandel's book *The Second Slump* (New Left Books, London, 1978) and is also discussed in G. Arrighi's article, 'Towards a Theory of Capitalist Crisis', *New Left Review*, no. 111 (1978), pp. 3-24; see also R. Rowthorn, 'Late Capitalism', *New Left Review*, no. 48 (1976), pp. 59-83. On social crisis tendencies, Habermas's book, *Legitimation Crisis* (Heinemann, London, 1976) is indispensable; see too J. Habermas, 'Conservatism and Capitalist Crisis', *New Left Review*, no. 115 (1979), pp. 73-84. Tom Nairn's studies of the cultural and political aspects of crisis formation are also important; see, for example, T. Nairn, *The Break-Up of Britain* (New Left Books, London, 1977) and T. Nairn, 'The Future of Britain's Crisis', *New Left Review*, nos. 113-14 (1979), pp. 43-69.

Regional Case Studies

Bagnasco, A. *Le tre Italie* (Il Mulino, Bologna, 1977)

Bagnasco, A. and Messori, M. *Tendenze dell'economia periferica* (Editoriale Valentino, Turin, 1975)

Barrot, J. *Languedoc-Roussillon – interventions de l'Etat et évolution de la crise régionale* (Economie et Politique, Paris, 1975)

Brown, G. (ed.) *Red Paper on Scotland* (EUSPB, Edinburgh, 1975)

Camagni, R.B. 'Il ruolo di un area sviluppata in condizioni di costo crescente di lavoro e del capitale: il caso della Lombardia', *Rivista Internazionale di Scienze Sociale*, no. 1 (1978)

Chapman, G. 'Theories of Development and Underdevelopment in Southern Italy', *Development and Change*, vol. 9 (1978), pp. 365-96

Chatou, G. 'Poitou-Charentes-l'industrialisation à la campagne', *Economie et Politique*, nos. 264-5 (July-August 1976)

Claussen, H. and Läpple, D. *Regionaluntersuchung Bremen* (Bremen, 1976).

Colin, A. and Cunat, F. 'Nord-Pas-de-Calais, face au gâchis généralisé', *Economie et Politique*, nos. 264-5 (1976), pp. 96-105

Damette, F. 'Crise urbaine et régionale de Marseille à Bordeaux', *Economie et Politique*, no. 195 (October 1970)

Damette, F. La région: un terrain neuf pour petites et grandes manoeuvres', *Economie et Politique*, no. 254 (September 1975), pp. 68-76

Dunford, M.F. 'Regional Policy and the Restructuring of Capital', *Working Paper 4* (Urban and Regional Studies, University of Sussex, 1977)

Fabre, E. 'Limousin – l'invisible main des monopoles', *Economie et Politique*, nos. 264-5 (1976)

Farrell, M. *Northern Ireland: the Orange State* (Pluto, London, 1976)

Garofoli, G. *Ristrutturazione industriale e territorio* (Agnelli, Milan, 1978)

Geraets, H. and Wegenwijs, F. 'Het Industrialisatieproces in Midden-Zeeland', *Zone*, no. 8 (1978), pp. 15-57

Graziani, A. *Investimenti Autonomi e Investimenti Indotti nell'Econ-*

omia del Mezzogiorno (University of Naples, Naples, 1977)

Graziani, A. 'The Mezzogiorno in the Italian Economy', *Cambridge Journal of Economics*, vol. 2 (1978), pp. 355-72

van Hoogstraten, P. and Kentgens, N. 'De Mijnstreek: enkele aspekten van regionale ontwikkeling', *Zone*, no. 1 (1976), pp. 8-99

Husson, J.C., and Toulon, C. 'Lorraine — la crise régionale n'est pas fatale', *Economie et Politique*, no. 171 (October, 1968)

Larsen, J. and Villadsen, S. (eds.) *Ulighed Mellem Regioner: Arbejds-papirer om den danske regionale udvikling* (Esbjerg, 1975)

Mutti, A. and Poli, I. *Sottosviluppo e Meridione* (Mazzotta, Milan, 1975)

Perrons, D. 'The Dialectic of Region and Class in Ireland', *Working Paper 8* (Urban and Regional Studies, University of Sussex, 1978)

Scheibling, J. 'Rhône-Alpes — croissance monopoliste, crise du CME et crises régionales', *Economie et Politique*, no. 239 (July 1974)

Secchi, B. *Squilibri regionali e sviluppo economico* (Marsilio, Padua, 1974)

NOTES ON CONTRIBUTORS

Felix Damette is a member of the European Parliament. He is a frequent contributor to *Economie et Politique*, as is Edmond Poncet. Felix Damette is also on the Editorial Board of this journal.

Dieter Läpple teaches at universities in Amsterdam, Eindhoven and Paris. He is a major contributor to the German debate on theories of the State.

Alain Lipietz researches at the Centre d'Etude Prospectives d'Economie Mathématique Appliqué à la Planification in Paris. His current work includes research on inflation and the inter-regional division of labour in service sector activities. He has recently published a major study *Crise et Inflation: Pourquoi?* (Maspero, 1979).

Pieter van Hoogstraten teaches at the University of Eindhoven. He is a frequent contributor to and member of the editorial board of *ZONE*.

Ray Hudson and *Jim Lewis* teach in the Geography Department of Durham University. *John Carney* is a researcher, associated with Durham University.

SUBJECT INDEX

LOCATION INDEX

AUTHOR INDEX